History Teaching with Moodle 2

Create a History course in Moodle packed with lessons and activities to make learning and teaching History interactive and fun

John Mannion

[PACKT] open source *
PUBLISHING   community experience distilled

BIRMINGHAM - MUMBAI

History Teaching with Moodle 2

First published: June 2011

Production Reference: 1090611

Published by Packt Publishing Ltd.
32 Lincoln Road
Olton
Birmingham, B27 6PA, UK.

ISBN 978-1-849514-04-0

www.packtpub.com

Cover Image by Charwak A. (charwak86@gmail.com)

Credits

Author
John Mannion

Reviewers
Mary Cooch

Kyle Goslin

Susan Smith Nash

Acquisition Editor
Sarah Cullington

Development Editor
Meeta Rajani

Technical Editor
Ajay Shanker

Project Coordinator
Vishal Bodwani

Proofreader
Lynda Sliwoski

Indexer
Hemangini Bari

Graphics
Nilesh R. Mohite

Production Coordinator
Kruthika Bangera

Cover Work
Kruthika Bangera

About the Author

John Mannion is from Manchester and has been a teacher in Primary and Secondary level education since September 1987, working in Manchester, Liverpool, and Madrid. He has worked at St. Gabriel's Independent Day School for Girls, Newbury, since January 1998. He is Head of ICT in Teaching & Learning and also teaches History.

I would like to thank my wife, Clare, and children, Louisa, Patrick, and Isobel for their understanding and encouragement. I owe a debt of gratitude to several professional colleagues whose contributions over the years have been inspirational – Jim and Anne Keogh, Sue Cocker, Ian Edwards, and Ben Lewis. The staff and pupils of St.Gabriel's have been wonderfully supportive, consistently providing invaluable feedback. Lastly, I would like to thank Sean and Josie, Mary, Ger, and Cath, my first teachers!

About the Reviewers

Mary Cooch is the author of *Moodle 2.0 First Look* and *Moodle 1.9 For Teaching 7-14 Year Olds*, also published by Packt Publishing. A languages and geography teacher for 25 years, Mary is based at Our Lady's High School, Preston, Lancashire, UK, but now spends part of her working week traveling Europe showing others how to make the most of this popular Virtual Learning Environment. Known online as the moodlefairy, Mary runs a blog on www.moodleblog.org and may be contacted for consultation via the training center based in her school, www.ourlearning.co.uk.

Kyle Goslin is a researcher and Ph.D. student at the Institute of Technology Blanchardstown, Dublin and has been researching and developing Moodle plug-ins and all things e-learning for the last number of years. Kyle's main areas of research are e-learning, user interaction, and enriching e-learning environments.

You can find his website and blog at http://www.kylegoslin.ie.

I would like to thank Dr. Markus Hofmann for introducing me to e-learning and Moodle and showing me how it's a platform for every idea.

Susan Smith Nash is currently Director of Education and Professional Development for the American Association of Petroleum Geologists (AAPG) in Tulsa, Oklahoma, and an adjunct professor at the University of Oklahoma. She was associate dean for graduate programs at Excelsior College (Albany, NY). Previous to that, she was online courses manager at Institute for Exploration and Development Geosciences, and director of curriculum development for the College of Liberal Studies, University of Oklahoma, Norman, OK, where she developed a degree program curriculum for online courses. She also developed interfaces for courses as well as administrative and procedural support, support programmers, protocol and training manuals, and marketing approaches. She obtained her Ph.D. and M.A. in English and a B.S. in Geology from the University of Oklahoma. Nash blogs at E-Learning Queen (`http://www.elearningqueen.com`) and E-Learners (`http://www.elearner.com`), and has written articles and chapters on mobile learning, poetics, contemporary culture, and e-learning for numerous publications, including *Trends and issues in instructional design and technology* (3rd ed.), *Mobile Information Communication Technologies Adoption in Developing Countries: Effects and Implications*, *Talisman*, *Press1*, *International Journal of Learning Objects*, *GHR*, *World Literature*, and *Gargoyle*. Her latest books include *Moodle 1.9 Teaching Techniques* (Packt Publishing, 2010), *E-Learners Survival Guide* (Texture Press, 2009), and *Klub Dobrih Dejanj* (2008).

I'd like to express my appreciation to Poorvi Nair for demonstrating the highest level of professionalism and project guidance.

www.PacktPub.com

Support files, eBooks, discount offers and more

You might want to visit www.PacktPub.com for support files and downloads related to your book.

Did you know that Packt offers eBook versions of every book published, with PDF and ePub files available? You can upgrade to the eBook version at www.PacktPub.com and as a print book customer, you are entitled to a discount on the eBook copy. Get in touch with us at service@packtpub.com for more details.

At www.PacktPub.com, you can also read a collection of free technical articles, sign up for a range of free newsletters and receive exclusive discounts and offers on Packt books and eBooks.

http://PacktLib.PacktPub.com

Do you need instant solutions to your IT questions? PacktLib is Packt's online digital book library. Here, you can access, read and search across Packt's entire library of books.

Why Subscribe?

- Fully searchable across every book published by Packt
- Copy and paste, print and bookmark content
- On demand and accessible via web browser

Free Access for Packt account holders

If you have an account with Packt at www.PacktPub.com, you can use this to access PacktLib today and view nine entirely free books. Simply use your login credentials for immediate access.

Table of Contents

Preface

Moodle is an e-learning platform that has transformed the way in which many teachers deliver their subject to students. Teachers who create courses for students can now build online versions with choices and possibilities that might not previously have existed. It has made this transition to online courses a straightforward and exciting process. The basic building blocks or modules such as forums, lessons, and workshops simply reflect good practice in the classroom. Moodle makes such tasks easier and more accessible. Other modules such as wikis, polls, chats, and databases encourage student collaboration and thus enhance the learning experience for students. Courses created with this technology provide reassurance to uncertain students and challenges to more able students.

What this book covers

Chapter 1, *Course Structure* looks at different course formats, effective use of labels, and the creation of a simple forum.

Chapter 2, *Create Attractive Courses* demonstrates how images and word clouds should be used to enhance course pages.

Chapter 3, *Adding Interactive Content* focuses on important procedures including uploading of files and creating links for students to submit work. A glossary is also created.

Chapter 4, *Quizzes* looks at different types of learning objects that can be created and also demonstrates good practice in organizing questions using categories and the question bank.

Chapter 5, *The Gradebook* looks at ways in which the Gradebook module enables teachers to replicate their markbook electronically and use it for the collation of reports, target setting, and more.

Chapter 6, Student Collaboration examines ways in which students can be encouraged to work and learn together. The chapter looks at wikis, polls, and databases.

Chapter 7, Lessons and Blogs covers modules that reinforce learning. The first module enables teachers to create exciting content that captures their expertise and the second enables students to pursue independent learning.

Chapter 8, Using Xerte and Audacity looks closely at two examples of open source software that enable teachers to add rich content to their Moodle courses.

Chapter 9, Moodle Workshops demonstrates how this important module empowers teachers and students to conduct meaningful and rewarding peer-to-peer assessments of work.

What you need for this book

You need access to:

- A local or online installation of Moodle 2.0
- A web browser such as Mozilla Firefox 3.6 or later, Internet Explorer v7 or later
- Gimp (image manipulation program) v2.6 or later
- Xerte v2.15 or later
- Audacity v1.2 or later
- Adobe Reader v9 or later

Who this book is for

This book is for History teachers who wish to make use of Moodle within their lesson plans and schemes of work. It is also suitable for aspiring and newly qualified teachers who are looking to extend their repertoire of skills at the chalkface! Teachers of any discipline would be able to extract ideas or improvise with the activities discussed in this book in order to add the constructive use of ICT to their teaching.

Conventions

In this book, you will find a number of styles of text that distinguish between different kinds of information. Here are some examples of these styles, and an explanation of their meaning.

Code words in text are shown as follows: "Enter the following formula:
=average([[5]],[[6]], [[7]])."

New terms and **important words** are shown in bold. Words that you see on the screen, in menus or dialog boxes for example, appear in the text like this: "We are going to use the **Topics** format in preference to the **Weeks** format or the **Social** format".

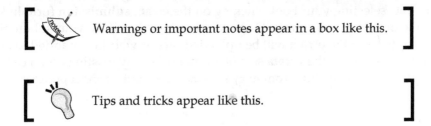

Warnings or important notes appear in a box like this.

Tips and tricks appear like this.

Reader feedback

Feedback from our readers is always welcome. Let us know what you think about this book—what you liked or may have disliked. Reader feedback is important for us to develop titles that you really get the most out of.

To send us general feedback, simply send an e-mail to feedback@packtpub.com, and mention the book title via the subject of your message.

If there is a book that you need and would like to see us publish, please send us a note in the **SUGGEST A TITLE** form on www.packtpub.com or e-mail suggest@packtpub.com.

If there is a topic that you have expertise in and you are interested in either writing or contributing to a book, see our author guide on www.packtpub.com/authors.

Customer support

Now that you are the proud owner of a Packt book, we have a number of things to help you to get the most from your purchase.

Errata

Although we have taken every care to ensure the accuracy of our content, mistakes do happen. If you find a mistake in one of our books — maybe a mistake in the text or the code — we would be grateful if you would report this to us. By doing so, you can save other readers from frustration and help us improve subsequent versions of this book. If you find any errata, please report them by visiting http://www.packtpub.com/support, selecting your book, clicking on the **errata submission form** link, and entering the details of your errata. Once your errata are verified, your submission will be accepted and the errata will be uploaded on our website, or added to any list of existing errata, under the **Errata** section of that title. Any existing errata can be viewed by selecting your title from http://www.packtpub.com/support.

Piracy

Piracy of copyrighted material on the Internet is an ongoing problem across all media. At Packt, we take the protection of our copyright and licenses very seriously. If you come across any illegal copies of our works, in any form, on the Internet, please provide us with the location address or website name immediately so that we can pursue a remedy.

Please contact us at copyright@packtpub.com with a link to the suspected pirated material.

We appreciate your help in protecting our authors, and our ability to bring you valuable content.

Questions

You can contact us at questions@packtpub.com if you are having a problem with any aspect of the book, and we will do our best to address it.

1
Course Structure

In classrooms far and wide vivid accounts of the Peasants' Revolt of 1381 and explanations of the siege engines of war are brought to life through the innovative use of ICT. The advent of Virtual Learning Environments (VLEs) in recent years has added a whole new dimension to the use of ICT in the teaching of History. One VLE in particular seems to have been created with History teachers in mind because of its ability to capture their enthusiasm and expertise and facilitate the creation of vivid and dynamic courses that mimic effective History teaching practice.

Moodle – Ideal for teaching History

Moodle, the VLE in question:

- Equips the History teacher with an array of tools that enhance good practice in the classroom
- Extends the learning of pupils beyond the lesson
- Creates opportunities to challenge the gifted and talented pupils
- Captures the individual teacher's expertise so that it can be reused by others
- Reinforces the learning that has taken place during a lesson
- Reassures students by reflecting their own use of ICT outside the classroom

Without being prescriptive in any way, Moodle brings together an arsenal of weapons to make the teaching of History even more exciting and relevant.

It enables a teacher to radically alter the pace of a lesson through the use of a quiz or a lesson. It challenges students to make informed judgments about the work of peers in forums, blogs, workshops, and interactive discussions. It creates opportunities for collaborative work in wikis and glossaries. It captures the expertise a teacher has to offer and makes it more accessible to:

- The quiet individual for whom the class debate is a struggle
- The enthusiast who needs a bit more reassurance to move up to the next level
- The talented child who finishes tasks but needs to develop the capacity to learn more independently

"History Teaching with Moodle" includes a number of assumptions, which I have made with confidence. The activities and ideas will appeal to good teachers, and it will enthuse the young teacher starting out in the profession. It will occasionally challenge the History technophobe to say, "Actually, that is not a bad idea!". Some of those mentioned above will spot Moodle's potential to harness skills and expertise and do something different with them. Others will quickly develop opportunities for themselves to be heard in conversations where it has not always been the case, in the staffroom or the classroom. And some will just pick up the ball, run with it, and see where it takes them.

One further assumption is that you are in a position to begin building a course. It could be an entire Key Stage 3 course about:

- The Medieval Period (Year 7)
- Renaissance, Reformation, and Revolution (Year 8)
- Empires and World Wars (Year 9)

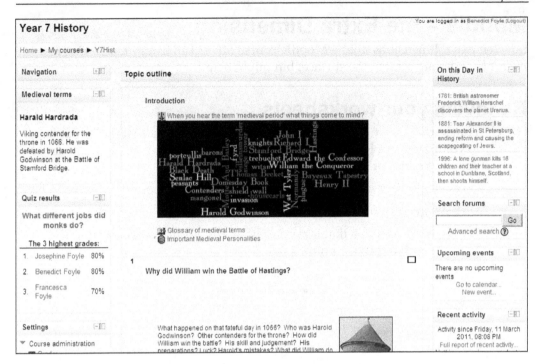

The course may reflect the new modular approach to teaching GCSE History. It could be based upon:

- The Divided Union looking at Post war USA, McCarthyism, Civil Rights, and so on

- The Germany 1918-1939 module

- Peace and War: International Relations 1901 - 1991

The institution may have its own Virtual Learning Environment but limited contributions from the History department. Courses may not have progressed much beyond using them to host resources. Readers will hopefully be in a position to take up the teacher role to create tasks and also to test them using student accounts. If this is not the case, then it is likely that having patiently read the book, readers will be in a strong position to beat down the Senior Management's door and demand some help in getting the ball rolling. As a consequence of reading this book, the relationship with your technicians in the ICT Department will alter dramatically as the nature of requests becomes more challenging and diverse. "Is it possible to try to do this?" sounds much more interesting to an ICT technician than, "*Please* could you fix this!".

Moodle – the Extra Dimension

So what extra dimensions does a Moodle course offer to a History teacher? A few examples can only scratch the surface, but might help.

Re-invent your worksheets

- Transform your information sheet about key individuals from the Russian Revolution into a Random Glossary (Chapter 3) in your course. This can be done in a series of stages.

- Create a glossary of the leading individuals from the period.

- Display an entry from the glossary on the front page.

- Set up the glossary so that it randomly selects a different entry from the glossary and displays it on the page.

Medieval terms

Harald Hardrada

Viking contender for the throne in 1066. He was defeated by Harold Godwinson at the Battle of Stamford Bridge.

Encourage students to collaborate

- Use a collaborative wiki (Chapter 6) to focus on improving answers to different types of examination questions

- Get students to write an answer to a particular question under examination conditions

- Mark the answer, giving it a Level such as Level 1

- Ask another student to improve it

- Use the History tab on the wiki to view the changes that are necessary to achieve the higher level answer

Get them using forums

- Use forums (Chapter 1) to enhance the quality of class debates

- Set an open ended question that demands a measured response from students

- Insist on use of sentences and paragraphs and refuse to accept 'textspeak'
- Encourage students to comment constructively on opposing arguments
- Use posts in a debate to raise the quality of the discussion
- Target the confident authors and engineer a situation where the same individual has to counter his/her own argument

---

When you hear the term 'medieval period' what things come to mind?
by John Mannion - Thursday, 23 December 2010, 10:54 PM

Please write in sentences. Do not use 'textspeak' or abbreviations.

Reply

Re: When you hear the term 'medieval period' what things come to mind?
by Benedict Foyle - Sunday, 13 March 2011, 08:16 PM

I like watching Robin Hood on the television. That is the medieval period. Last year I played Will Scarlet in our school production and it was really good. I liked the engines of war that you can see at Caerphilly Castle and it was really good looking at the Great Hall there.

Show parent | Reply

You are logged in as Francesca Foyle (Logout)

History teachers are familiar with open-ended questions that bring the subject to life in discussion, debate, and presentation. The same questions can be put to work alongside Moodle's tools to provide a dynamic learning experience for students. They can evaluate each other's work in a workshop or investigate key features of an event in a lesson, quiz, or wiki. The permutations are endless and the opportunities for History teachers in particular, are mouth watering.

- Year 7, Medieval Period: What was the single most important reason for William's victory at Hastings?
- Year 8, Renaissance, Reformation, and Revolution: Was Mary Tudor really such a bad queen?
- Year 9, Empires and World Wars: Was the Empire a good or a bad thing?
- Year 10, Germany 1918 -1939: Was the Reichstag fire the main reason why Hitler was able to establish a dictatorship in Germany in 1934?

- Year 11, Cold War and International Relations: What was the main reason why Khruschev decided to place missiles in Cuba in 1962?

Creative use of tools within Moodle provides opportunities to get even more out of students because they recognize the value of the tools. Forums help them to concentrate on one reason why Hitler came to power whilst studying a collection of other reasons provided by their peers. They are thus more equipped to answer that detailed question which asks them to discuss at least three reasons and prioritize the most important.

Similarly, it becomes easier to compose an examination answer that requires explanation and discussion of more than one reason why Khruschev decided to deploy missiles in Cuba in 1962. The same forum becomes an ideal focal point for revision on the Cuban missile crisis. Students learn by doing and forums, wikis, lessons, and workshops allow them to do more whilst notionally appearing to do less. By embracing the way students use technology in everyday life, teachers are allowing them to learn in a collaborative way and in fact helping them to achieve more than they might if they simply wrote up notes from a textbook.

Your first History course

Where to start? The best place is with a scheme of work for a particular year group. Start by building one course and acquiring particular skills. This will inevitably lead on to creating other courses so that those skills can be enhanced and utilized with other year groups.

Key stage 3 courses (11 – 13 year olds)

We are going to create a course for a Year 7 group using a list of key questions, which a teacher might plan to cover in a year. Using this format, it is possible to create a course that has the appropriate structure. For example the Year 7 course might cover the following questions over the academic year:

1. Why did William win the Battle of Hastings?
2. What did medieval people believe?
3. What was life like for medieval peasants?
4. What was the impact of the Black Death?
5. Why did the peasants revolt in 1381?
6. Who was the best king: Henry II, Richard I, or John?
7. How did castles work?

8.   How did explorers discover the rest of the world?

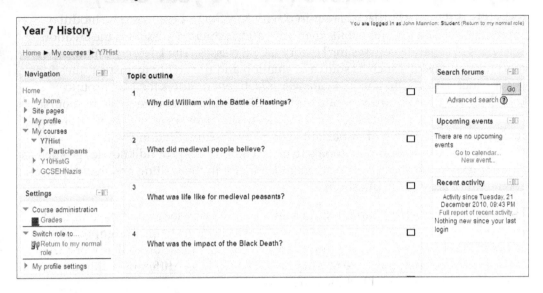

Schemes of work such as this lend themselves to the creation of a single course. Students tend to like the fact that everything they have covered in the year can be found under one roof and they appreciate the benefits to their revision. They have their exercise books to revise from but the course also provides them with the opportunity to revisit quizzes, video clips, slides that reinforce their understanding, and wikis that demonstrate how to answer particular types of questions effectively.

All the topics for the year will be placed in this course. Students will develop their essay writing skills with the emphasis on style and use of their own knowledge. We can use Moodle to highlight and evaluate examples of good practice in a workshop. Students will also work with sources and evaluate their usefulness. As with a book, the resources will be kept in one place but unlike a book the variety of sources that can be used is much more varied and extensive. A collaborative wiki can be set up so that students learn to empathize with medieval peasants or monks. We can use the book module to ensure that any notes about a particular topic are easily accessible. We can set up links to other sites so that independent learners can pursue their own line of enquiry. The series of eight questions create logical sections within our course. During the course, specific tasks and activities will be assessed such as the essay, sources exercises, and quizzes. The gradebook will record student performance. Marking and feedback will be provided in line with the institution's marking policy.

Key stage 4 courses (14 – 16 year olds)

A slightly different approach is required with Key Stage 4 courses. The modular approach, tackling different skills in examination papers necessitates the creation of a series of separate courses for History GCSE classes. The Divided Union paper concentrates on skills such as source evaluation and the ability to answer questions of a distinct nature. Obviously, to answer effectively requires the background knowledge to the McCarthy period and the Civil Rights movement. Such a course would concentrate on teaching how to write model answers as well as reinforcing students' understanding of important content and issues. Students will find in the course an array of learning materials to ensure good background knowledge such as quizzes, lessons, flashcards, and so on and practice in the writing and evaluating of good quality answers to questions.

The Germany 1918-1939 paper requires an in-depth knowledge and the ability to write good answers to causation questions. A good course helps to signpost strong technique and prepare students thoroughly for the examination so that when they come to sit the paper, there are no surprises. The skills are different within the courses and the courses reflect the differences.

Students at this key stage are able to cope with a greater number of courses in their subject. In History, they also appreciate that the series of questions allows them to breakdown and learn the content and the different techniques required to achieve the higher grades. If they want to work on their ability to answer causation questions then a good course will have clear signposts to the differences between a Level 1, 2, and 3 answer (use a wiki), quizzes, flashcards, notes, and so on to cover key content (examples in each course section), and opportunities to submit answers to workshops and to teaching staff.

There are clear differences between courses at Years 7 and 8 compared to Years 10 and 11. Moodle caters for the difference in needs and the concentration on content or a skills-based approach. Teachers will recognize and share these aspirations. Moodle enhances the way teachers do it at the moment. The Moodle course is another vital component to success alongside the exercise book and folder, the lever arch file, and the textbook.

Naming your course

Before the course can be put together, there are a number of issues that need to be decided upon. Our plan is to create a course called **Year 7 History** in the **History** category and it will have the course code **Y7Hist**. It will consist of eight topics and we plan to build it gradually so that by the end of the course it contains a rich seam of resources, tasks, and activities but also contains clear signposts to the skills that we want the Year 7 classes to practice this year. There will be a series of tasks and activities that will be recorded in the gradebook for the course to indicate student levels of attainment and to help with report writing. We plan to concentrate on interpreting and evaluating sources, exercises in empathy, and essay writing techniques.

We are going to use the **Topics** format in preference to the **Weeks** format or the **Social** format. We shall look at these two formats later in the chapter. Suffice to say the **Topics** format allows us to select how many topics we want visible on the home page and allows this figure to be adjusted. We also need to consider how we wish to make the course available to students. Initially, whilst we are setting it up we could make it impossible for students to enroll in it. We plan to assign students to the course ourselves so that we are in complete control of this important aspect. We shall then invite students to post an entry into a forum in answer to an open-ended question about their understanding of the term 'medieval'.

Creating the History category

1. Creating the **History** category is straightforward if you have administrator rights, log in as administrator.Click **Site Administraton** in the left-hand pane.

2. Click **Courses**.

3. Click **Add/edit courses**.

4. Click the **Add new category** button.

5. Enter **History** in the **Category Name** textbox.

6. Click the **Add a new course** button.

Create the Year 7 History course

This will initiate the **Course Settings** window. The first part of the window covers the settings we have previously discussed. The course summary will appear alongside the link to the course on the student's home page. Take note of the location for selecting the course format and the number of topics.

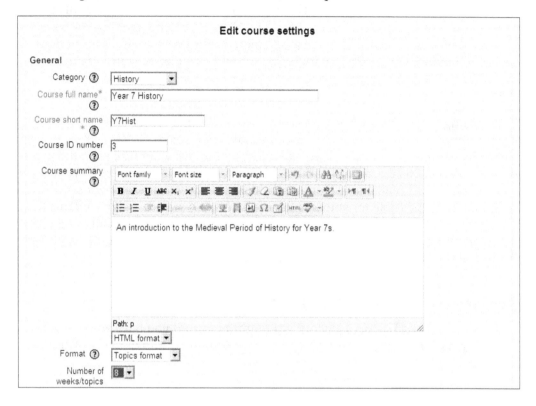

Further down the page, there are more settings that need to be negotiated.

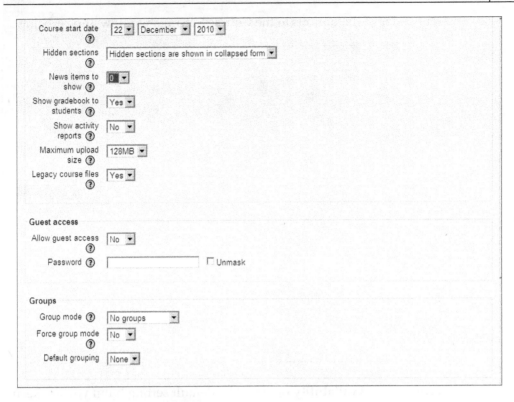

1. We have left the first two sections at their default values.

2. We have set **News items to show** as 0 because we do not want the **Latest News** block to appear on the home page. We shall deal with blocks in more detail in the next chapter.

3. We do want students to be able to see the **Gradebook**, which we shall look at in more detail in Chapter 5.

4. We shall discuss **activity reports** in detail when we look at how Moodle can assist with report writing and parent consultations.

5. We have set **Legacy Course files** to **Yes** because this is an important concession to file management in earlier versions of Moodle. The new approach adopted under Moodle 2 may not be to everyone's taste. More of this when we look at uploading of files in the next chapter.

6. **Guest access** we have left at their default settings.

7. **Groups** have been left at their default settings for now although this will change as we investigate this aspect in a later chapter.

8. The remainder of the options in the **Course Settings** window appear below:

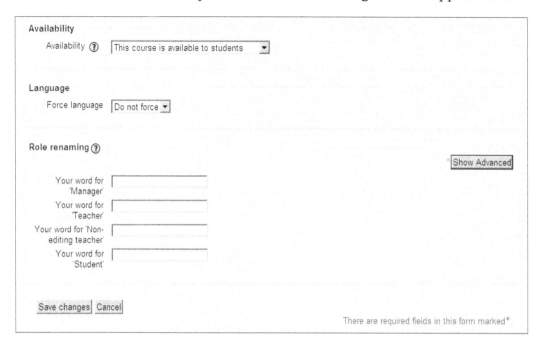

9. We have left the **Availability** option at its default setting but if you are keen to avoid students logging in to the course before you are ready, you may prefer to set it to **This course is not available to students**.

10. We have left the remaining settings at their default values.

11. Click **Save changes**.

Creating and enrolling users

Completion of the **Course Settings** window immediately takes you to the next stage of the process when setting up a course for the first time – enrolling teachers and students.

Creating users

If you saved changes at the end of the **Course Settings** window, you will see an option in the next screen to **Add a new user**. If not, this option is available if you do the following:

1. Click **Site Administration** in the left-hand pane.

2. Click **Users**.

3. Click **Accounts**.

4. Click **Add a new user**.

5. In this section, the fields that are essential are marked with an asterisk. If you do not have administrator rights then it is highly unlikely that you will be able to create users yourself. However, when you have been assigned the role of a teacher for a course, you will be able to assign students to your course.

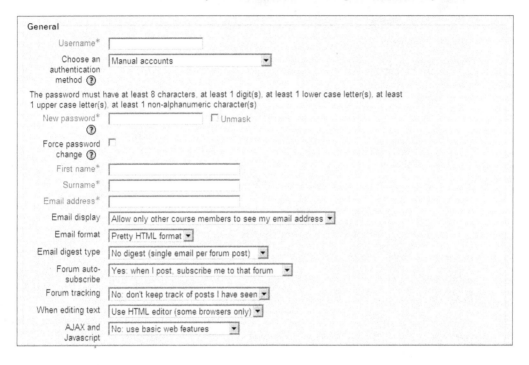

6. Enter values in the fields marked with an asterisk and leave the remaining fields at their default values. Do not forget the town and country fields midway down the page.

7. Click the **Update profile** button.

8. Repeat this procedure to add some more students and teachers.

9. Click **Browse list of users** to see a list of the users you have created.

Enrol users

As administrator, you have the ability to enrol users in courses.

1. Click **Course administration**.
2. Click **Users**.
3. Click **Enrolled users**.
4. In the **Enrolment method** select **Manual enrolments**.
5. Click **Enrol users**.
6. Select **teacher** or **student** from the drop-down menu.
7. Click the **Enrol** button.
8. The screen will refresh with the new users added to the table.

It is highly likely that you find yourself in the position of working for an establishment where Moodle has been set up and already has an administrator whose job it is to create courses and create users. In this case, the previous three sections will have been of limited value. Still, you need to create a Year 7 History course and here are some suggestions as to how to go about it.

* Contact the Moodle administrator at your establishment.
* Confirm your Moodle username and password with your administrator.
* Inform the administrator that you would like to set up a Moodle course in History for your Year 7 group.
* Request that you be assigned the role of 'teacher' within the course.
* Negotiate a name for the course with the administrator. There may be a strict naming policy in place so 'Murder, Mayhem and Madness' may have to be sacrificed for something more prosaic such as 'Year 7 History'.
* Ask if you can watch the process take place. This procedure takes seconds. You will see where the course is placed within the existing structure and this will enable you to access the course easily once you are on your own. You will also see yourself assigned the role of 'teacher' within the course.

Log in to the establishment's Moodle, preferably with the course creator still alongside and navigate to the course. The suggestions may seem pedantic but they ensure that you have a clear route through to your course once you have to do it alone.

Having confirmed that the course exists, revisit the notes in the section about enrolling students and see if you can assign students to your course. Check also that you can access the **Course Settings** page and find the particular setting that prevents those students from accessing your course until you are absolutely ready to allow them in.

If student Benedict Foyle were to log in to the new Year 7 History course in our Moodle, he would see the following screen:

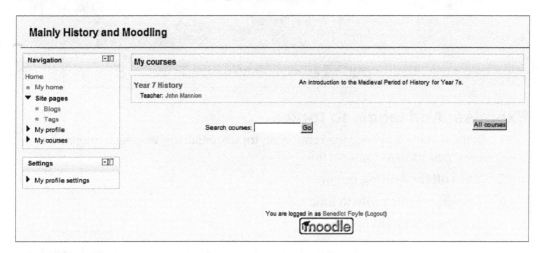

Having reached this point, the shackles are off and you are ready to start working on your first Moodle course.

Adding topic labels

The first thing we are going to do is to add the eight questions as headings in topic labels. In the following chapter, we will return to the labels and look at how to add images and use the labels more effectively to signpost to students what will be covered in each section.

1. Log in to your moodle with your username and password.
2. Click on the link to **Year 7 History**, which should be clearly visible if you have been assigned as a teacher to this course.
3. Click the **Turn editing on** button.
4. Click the **Edit Summary** symbol in the section for Topic 1.
5. Uncheck the box headed 'Use default section name'.
6. This activates the **Section name** textbox where you can type the first of the topic headings 'Why did William win the Battle of Hastings?'.
7. Leave the **Description** box blank for now.
8. Click **Save Changes**.

Topic 1 should appear as in the following screenshot:

Exercise: Add labels to topics

1. Repeat steps 4 to 8 for the remaining topics, ensuring that each question is assigned its own topic section.

2. Turn off the **Editing** button.

3. Click the **Switch role to** link.

4. Select the **Student** option.

The course should now appear as in the following screenshot. This is what a student would see if he or she went into the course as it stands at present. Note the reference in the top right-hand corner to my role as a student in this view.

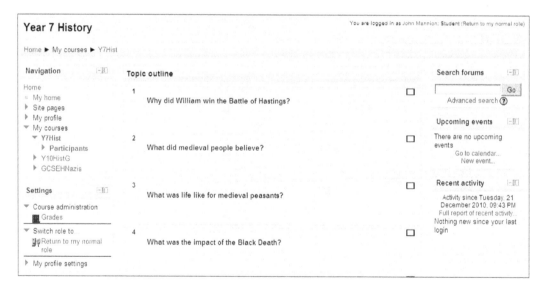

○ Before starting the next task, you need to ensure that you have clicked on the link to **Return to my normal role**.

Your first forum

A forum is an ideal way to get students involved in a course. Setting an open-ended question for which there is no right or wrong answer encourages them to set down their ideas clearly. Giving them some guidelines about expectations is important. Do not permit the use of "text-speak" or abbreviations. Ideally, posts should be in sentences and paragraphs. Pupils like forums; the quiet ones find that they have an equal voice and that their opinions carry as much weight as their more outspoken peers. It is also a good way to get a feel for what the group understands about a particular topic, and any misconceptions they may have.

Use open-ended questions

We are going to open up a simple forum where students can respond to the question, "When you hear the term 'medieval period' what things come to mind?" Similar open-ended questions could be added to courses for other year groups:

- What was the main reason for Henry VIII's break from Rome? (Year 8)
- "Lions led by Donkeys!" How fair is this assessment of the role of the generals in WW1? (Year 9)
- Were improved wages the main effect of the Nazis economic policies? (Year 10)
- Why did relations between the Soviet Union and the USA change between 1943 and 1956? (Year 11)

Types of forum

Having established clearly the question that you want to set and what your expectations are of your students, it is time to set up the first forum. There are several types of forum from which to choose. We shall use the **single, simple discussion**.

Setting up a forum

The ideal location for your first forum is in the top unnamed section above Topic 1.

1. Enter the **Year 7 History** course and turn editing on.
2. Click on the **Add an activity** dropdown in the top section above **Topic 1**.
3. Select **Forum** from the list.

4. Enter the values as shown in the following screenshot:

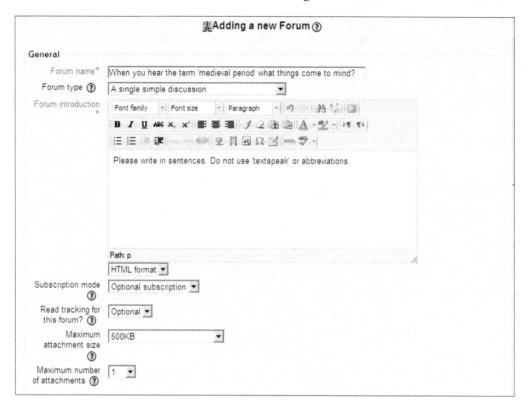

 ° The Forum name is crucial because this is the hyperlink that students will spot on the course page. It should be unambiguous. Use the forum introduction to set out your expectations of the students. There are some things that can never be repeated enough times! We have left the **Subscription mode** as optional because we do not necessarily want them to receive e-mail copies of each post for this. Students may wish to upload an image that they feel is relevant to the discussion.

 ° The **Post threshold for blocking** section allows you to deal with over enthusiastic users who post too many responses to the question. Default settings apply in this case.

 ° We will look at **Grade**, **Ratings**, and **Common module settings** in more detail in the relevant chapters. The only setting we have altered is the ID no. of 1 for this activity because it is the first task we have asked the students to do.

5. Click **Save and return to course**.

6. Click **Turn editing off**.
7. Click **Switch role to**.
8. Select **student**.
9. Click the forum hyperlink in the top section and you should see something similar to the following screenshot:

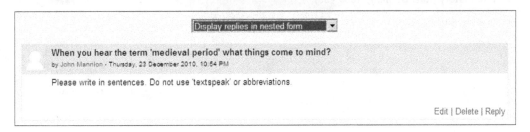

Notice that students have a variety of options to display the posts in the dropdown box at the top and the links to post their replies can be found in the bottom corner.

Exercise: Course creation

Try this exercise to test out the skills you have acquired this far:

1. Create a course called Year 10 History (Nazi Germany 1930-39) with the course code Y10HistG. Assign yourself as a teacher to the course and also assign some students. (You may need to consult your administrators in order to do this.) Use the 'Topic' format in the Format section.

2. It is a nine-topic course and the key questions covered over the duration of the course are as follows:
   ° How did Hitler come to power?
   ° How did Hitler move from Chancellor to Fuhrer?
   ° How did Hitler keep Germany under control?
   ° How did Hitler cut unemployment?
   ° How did Hitler control the minds of the young?
   ° What was the role of women in Nazi Germany?
   ° What were Hitler's relations with the Church like?
   ° Was there opposition from groups like the Communists, Catholics, army officers, and students?
   ° How did Nazi policies against the Jews develop in the period 1933-39?

3. Set up a forum with the question *'What did followers of Nazism believe?'*

4. Ask students to respond to the question in sentences and avoid the use of text-speak.

When it is finished, the page a student will see should resemble the following screenshot:

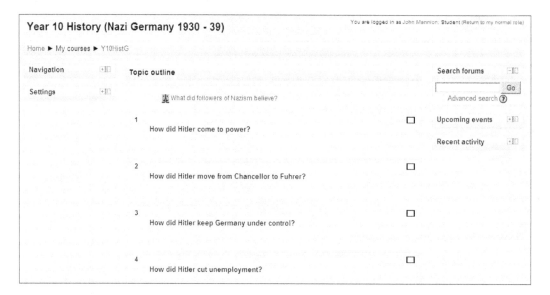

Clio's Challenge – a social format

As the name suggests, this format is useful for those courses that might need to resemble a brochure or magazine in terms of content. For example, there may be a History society in school or a Challenge and Extension group. This course format concentrates on presenting and exchanging information with members. The main body of the page consists of a social forum. It dominates the center pane and several blocks along the side panes can be used to present relevant information to visitors.

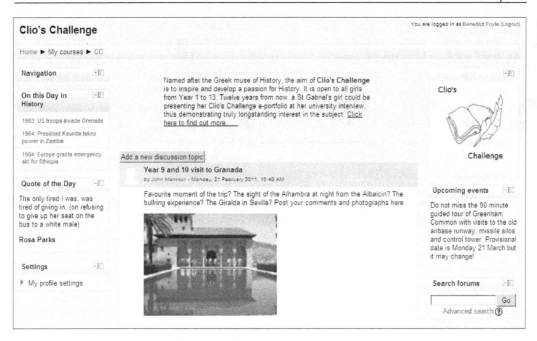

Clio's Challenge is the brain child of an inspirational colleague who wanted to open up History to the entire age range. She achieved it by challenging pupils of all ages to record their passion for History in different ways. It could, for example, be in the form of:

- A book review of a historical novel
- A podcast about a visit to a place of historical interest during holiday
- A blog entry about a recent radio or TV program

Younger pupils meeting the challenge through this form of independent learning could earn house points and certificates to demonstrate their love of History. Equally, a student who is at the point of applying to study History at university could point to a love of the subject that clearly predates the years of public examinations.

Clio's Challenge is in a social format because it is not prescriptive in any way. Pupils offer ideas and share advice and tips about meeting the challenges. Useful experiences can be recorded there and relevant documents made available. Work can be posted, viewed, and commented upon by peers, teachers, and mentors.

The screenshot shows the use of an HTML block to summarize the raison d'etre of the club. It also includes **RSS feeds** which provide relevant, ever changing links. We shall look at how to set up RSS feeds in Chapter 3. They provide an invaluable opportunity to relate your class teaching to current events. Be prepared, for example, to interrupt your plans in order to explain the meaning of 'Dunkirk spirit' to inquisitive twelve year olds who spot an important anniversary and need to know more. Once the RSS link is set up, the course refreshes the links on a regular basis without any need for intervention. Quote of the Day could be another **RSS feed** or it could be a collection of quotes which have been transformed into a **Random Glossary**. We shall also look at these features in Chapter 3.

A **Social forum** is therefore a departure from the topic- or week-based structure that we have looked at this far. It clearly has a place because it can act as a focal point for extra- curricular activities, and it is also a logical place to give more wide ranging permissions and responsibilities to pupils with the motivation to do that little bit extra.

Summary

In this chapter, we have introduced the idea that Moodle is a superb platform on which to base a significant element of your History teaching. If your students need supplementary assistance beyond the exercise books, folders, and textbooks then it lends itself to this. If challenging and extending your brightest students is an issue for you then Moodle is packed with opportunities to develop their independent learning skills. If you want to develop their ability to collaborate in their learning to drive up standards and expectations, then this piece of software makes it possible. Key to any success is the drive and desire of the individual teacher to apply knowledge and expertise and so make tasks and activities relevant, rewarding, and meaningful. We have:

- Looked at some different course formats such as topic, weekly and social that are available to teachers when they embark upon building their first courses
- Discussed how to set up courses and enrol students
- Created a simple forum that draws pupils to the course at an early stage
- Added labels to a course that can now can be adapted, extended, and moulded to produce interactive, reflective, and collaborative forms of learning

In the next chapter, we shall look at the use of images to make the course more attractive and appealing. We shall also add features to the course that change frequently, thus creating the impression of a vibrant and dynamic course.

2
Create Attractive Courses

The use of images in a Moodle course is vital. It can make or break the course as far as students are concerned. They are used to web pages appearing seamlessly on screen with innovative use of images that immediately grab their attention. This does not mean that you have to go on the next available Photoshop course but it is important to bear in mind certain fundamentals when selecting images to use on your Moodle course. They can do so much more than simply help to break up the text and give each topic or weekly section a separate identity. Images, used sensibly and creatively can enhance a course page and profoundly influence the success of the learning process. Images can spark debate, reinforce understanding, lead to a deeper level of questioning among students, and enhance the learning process.

In this chapter, we are going to look at how the careful selection and manipulation of images can enable greater understanding of the features of medieval castles. A selection of eight images will be placed in the **Topic** sections of the course. The images will be the same size and will provide an element of continuity as students look at the course. What has an image of crenellations got to do with 'What medieval people believed?' What has an image of a portcullis got to do with the Peasants Revolt? In a sense they are all connected by the study of the medieval period. My images will reinforce the understanding of castles as not only defensive installations, but also as a hugely significant means of control of the local area and population.

This idea could apply to other courses. The Divided Union course for Year 11s could include an image of a significant character from each particular section. Post war America could have an image of President Eisenhower, The McCarthyism section could use Senator Joe McCarthy as its image, and so on. The Montgomery Bus Boycott could use Rosa Parks. Careful selection of appropriate images reinforces understanding for students. Taking the time to alternate images on a regular basis is a useful way of reinforcing their ability to identify key individuals.

In a Russian Revolution course, you can use the selection of topic questions and regularly change the image associated with particular key questions. A topic such as 'Why was there a revolution in 1917?' lends itself to a host of images of key individuals who were of significance. Changing the image associated with that particular topic provides an opportunity to question students as to the identity of the individual and why he/she is important. It is not just there to break up the text. It becomes an important aide memoire, a prompt, and a means of supporting students and keeping the contents of each topic fresh in their minds because a couple of minutes are spent discussing something relevant to the course. 'Why did the Reds win the Civil War?' could use images not just of Lenin and Trotsky but the various White Generals with chronic addictions to drugs and alcohol and lack of a coherent strategy. It clearly impresses examiners when students can identify key individuals in picture sources, use correct spellings, and when they can provide evidence of their own knowledge. This approach lends itself to that end and is quite easy to achieve. In this chapter, we will:

- Manipulate images to make them ready for use on a page
- Upload single images
- Upload groups of images
- Use images and labels to improve the look and feel of course pages
- Display a directory of images

Preparing images

There are lots of different ways of collecting images for use on the course page. You can take photographs and use image editing software to crop sections that can then be inserted alongside the various topic sections of the home page. A finished topic section might resemble the following screenshot. You can align the images so that they appear underneath each other by topic or week with fully justified text to the left. There are lots of variations depending upon your own preferences.

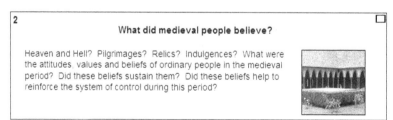

You might for example, prefer to situate the images in different positions within the topics and align any text accordingly. It is worth following the procedure to create this effect before exploring different ways of making the course page look attractive and inviting for students.

Collecting images

GIMP software is useful for editing photographic images. GIMP is an open source piece of image editing software. Being open source, it is free to download from the following site: http://uberdownloads.net. Further details about GIMP are available from this site. There are other free image editing tools available and you may have a particular favorite. In terms of what you need to be able to do with images for use on your Moodle course, you need to be able to crop images easily, scale images to an exact size without losing proportions, and save images in one of the formats that are necessary for web-based software such as Moodle. If your image editing software can save your digital photos in gif, jpg, or png formats then it will be suitable for our purposes. Picasa is a web-based alternative to GIMP and has the advantage that it can also be used to host your collection of images.

The following sections look at how to perform the list of tasks outlined to prepare images for use with a Moodle course. This section assumes that you have obtained your free version of GIMP for the following set of activities.

Cropping an image using GIMP

We need to take a digital photograph and prepare a square-shaped image from it. If your preference is for landscape or portrait-shaped images, the procedure is identical as long as you take into account the differing widths and heights.

1. Open GIMP.
2. Open the image you wish to crop.
3. Click **Tools**.
4. Click **Transform Tools**.
5. Select **Crop** from the list.
6. Click and drag the required selection.
7. Double-click on the image selection when satisfied that this is the image that is required.
    ° The dimensions of your selection are clearly visible on the taskbar.
    ° Small adjustments can be made to image selection by clicking and dragging on one of the sides to adjust it to the exact measurement that reflects your square, landscape, or portrait shape. For our purposes, we shall select only square shapes for the course page.

Scaling an image using GIMP

We need to scale the image to the precise size it must be in order to be inserted onto the course page. We do not want to distort our original selection. Ignoring this section may result in your image being too large and the downloading of the image may take an inordinate amount of time thus dissuading students from continuing with the task of looking at the course page. A suitable size for such images is 100 X 100 pixels. Pixels are the smallest measurement available for images, each pixel representing a color dot on the computer screen. You may use other measurements such as mm, cm, inches, and so on.

1. Click **Image**.
2. Click **Scale image**.

3. In the dialog box, enter the values required for the scaled image.
4. Click the **Scale** button.

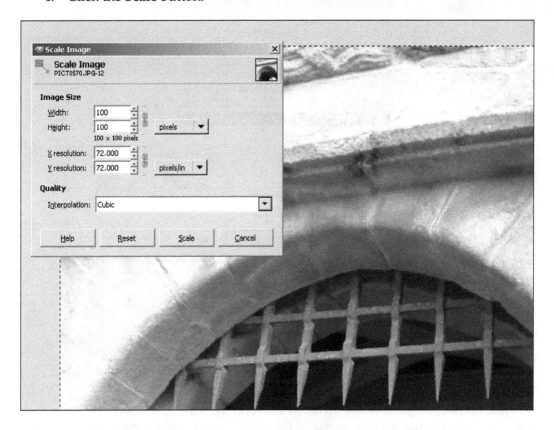

Saving an image using GIMP

As indicated earlier, it is important to save an image for use in Moodle with the correct file format. Bmp is not a suitable file format as sizes tend to be too large and take too long to download. The file formats to use with your Moodle pages are gif, jpg, and png. The latter two are for use with photographic images. The png format is suitable for this type of work because files appear on the page quickly and the quality is not compromised.

1. Click **File**.
2. Click **Save As**.
3. Give the image an appropriate filename.

4. In the dialog box, select a location for the file.

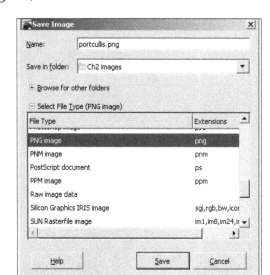

5. Expand the **Select FileType** option.
6. Select the png format.
7. Click **Save**.
8. Accept any default settings and select the **Export** option.
9. Click **Save** again.

We must repeat the procedures involved in cropping, scaling, and saving for each individual image that we plan to use. If this seems like a rather time consuming and unnecessary task, it really is not. As with any process in Moodle, if you invest the time initially it really does become second nature later on. And these are procedures that we will use many times in the creation of courses. We also have to consider that if we have gathered together suitable digital images then it is a shrewd use of time if we prepare them properly for effective use in our course. The look of any course is crucial and first impressions count. If students like the look and feel then they will return to it and make use of the course. If it looks like a dog's dinner then their approach may be less purposeful than we had intended.

We should save our images to a named folder such as Yr7HistCastleImages. Our images are now ready to be used within the course page.

Working with images

We are going to look at how to upload a single image for use with the 'What did medieval people believe?' topic section of our course page. We are going to place it within a label on the right-hand side and to the left of it there will be text explaining in detail what this particular topic will cover. We shall then look at how to upload a folder of images so that they can be used in the same way with other topic sections. A key point about the process we are now going to follow is that it is exactly the same process if we are trying to upload any type of file. Uploading a file with a .png extension is exactly the same as uploading word processed documents with .odt or .doc extensions, spreadsheet files with .xls extensions, audio files with .wmv or .mp3 extensions, and video files with .flv extensions.

Inserting a label

To start our work on the course page, we need to make use of a label. Labels are a means by which we create effective signposts on our course page. They offer the opportunity to create quite dramatic signposts if that is your forte. We are going to create a label containing text about this topic and an image of a portcullis on the right-hand side that is 100 X 100 pixels.

1. Open the **Yr 7 History** course and turn editing on.

2. Click the **Add a resource** dropdown in the **Topic Summary** 'What did medieval people believe?'.

3. Select the Label option.

4. Click the **Insert/edit image** button.

5. Click **Find or upload an image**.

6. Click **Upload a file**.

7. Click the **Browse** button.

8. Navigate to the correct image, select it, and confirm that the correct image has appeared in the **Attachment** textbox.

9. Give the image an appropriate filename and include its extension such as portcullis.jpg.

10. Click **Upload this file**.

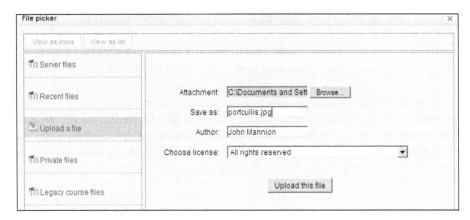

Preparing the image

How do we position the image on the right-hand side of the label? How do we add text on the left-hand side? How do we ensure that the label looks neat and tidy? All of these questions are answered within the General, Appearance, and Advanced tabs that are visible when the image is uploaded.

General tab

1. Enter a suitable description for the portcullis in the **Image description** textbox.

This text will appear as a tool tip when the mouse is hovered over the image—a useful opportunity to add extra information for the user about the image. Not all browsers will show the tool tip. There is no limit to the amount of detail you can type in this textbox.

2. Click the **Appearance** tab.

Appearance tab

In this tab, it is possible to make important choices about the position of the image and how the text behaves around it.

3. Select **Right** in the **Alignment** dropdown.

4. Set **Vertical** and **Horizontal** space to **0**.

5. Set **Border** to **1**.

6. Click the **Insert** button.

We have set the image as close to the edges of the label as possible and placed a thin black border around the image.

7. Click the **Advanced** tab.

Advanced tab

This tab provides more options to influence the behavior of the image. For example we could create an effect whereby the image switches to an alternative image when the mouse moves over the original image and switches back again when the mouse is withdrawn from the image. Imagine a Topic Section about causes of the Russian Revolution where the image switches between Tsar Nicholas II, Lenin, and Rasputin as the mouse moves over and back again.

8. Click the **Update** button.

Adding text to a label

We can now add text to the left-hand side of the label. The text should offer a clear indication of the content of the section. Students will look to this text expectantly when starting a topic for the first time and will look for clarity when doing revision. I mentioned signposts. Maybe this section is where you concentrate on how to answer causation questions with model answers and wikis showing a Level 1 answer can become a Level 2 or a Level 3 answer. The text has to be considered carefully.

1. Click on the text area.
2. The cursor will appear to the left of the image.
3. Enter the text in the space available.
4. Click **Save and return to course**.
5. Turn off editing to see how the label looks on the course page.

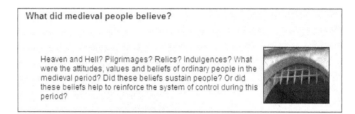

What did medieval people believe?

Heaven and Hell? Pilgrimages? Relics? Indulgences? What were the attitudes, values and beliefs of ordinary people in the medieval period? Did these beliefs sustain people? Or did these beliefs help to reinforce the system of control during this period?

Uploading multiple files

We have a folder containing several other images, which could be used for the remaining topic sections. Do we have to upload the images one by one? The logical place to store the selection of images would be within the Year 7 History course. That way the image files could be easily reused. In the next chapter we shall create a Glossary, a dictionary of terms appropriate to the course. Students can look up a particular term by searching for it within the Glossary. It will include terms such as moat, portcullis, and drawbridge as well as other terms relevant to the course such as Harald Hardrada, Domesday Book, and Witan. A relevant image would help to clarify a student's understanding of the term he or she was actually looking up.

The images can also be used in a variety of other tasks that we shall look at including lessons, quizzes, polls, databases, and wikis. We now need to look at the process of uploading multiple files.

Creating a zipped folder

Moodle allows you to upload a zipped file. A zipped folder is one that has been compressed or made smaller in order to make the transfer of the folder easier. This is more convenient than having to go through the earlier process of image uploading several times. Windows XP allows me to create a zipped file quite easily.

1. Right-click the folder **Yr7HistoryCastle Images**.

2. Select **Send To**.

3. Select **Compressed (zipped) Folder**.

4. A zipped folder with the same name but a **.zip** extension (and a zip fastener!) appears.

This is the folder that we shall upload to the **Year7 History** course.

Uploading a zipped folder

Moodle allows zipped folders to be uploaded to courses. The trick is to then unzip the folder so that it appears as the original folder. The zipped folder can then be discretely removed and the images folder can be used and reused throughout the course. We are going to place the folder in the top section of the course underneath our first forum.

1. Open the Yr 7 History course and turn editing on.

2. In the Top section, click on the **Add a resource** dropdown.

3. Select **Folder**.

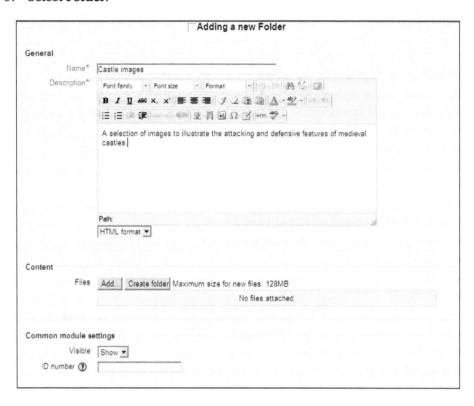

-   °   We have given the folder a distinctive name because this will become the hyperlink that students see and we have added a useful description of the contents.

4. Click the **Add** button.
5. In the File picker window, click **Upload a file**.
6. Using the **Browse** button, navigate to the zipped folder you intend to use.
7. Click the **Upload this file** button.

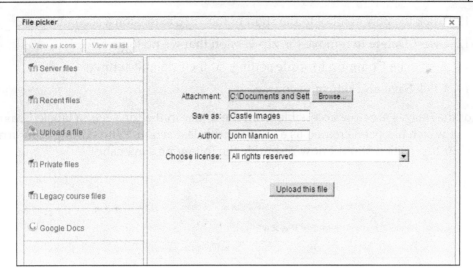

- In the **Content** section, the zipped folder is now clearly visible with a new symbol to the right of it.

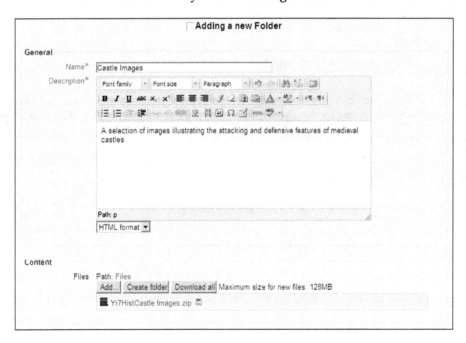

8. Click the new symbol to the right of the `.zip` extension.

9. Select **Unzip**.

10. The `Year7HistCastle Images` folder should appear above the zip version.

11. Click the new symbol to the right of the `.zip` extension a second time.

12. Select **Delete** to remove the zip version that we no longer need.

13. Leave the **Common Module** settings at their default settings.

14. Click **Save and return to course.**

All of the images are now accessible from the folder in the top section labeled `Castle Images` which has been created as a result of this last action. With editing still turned on, your top section should now resemble the following screenshot:

What do the six symbols on the same line as the `Castle Images` folder stand for? You should have noticed that they appear and disappear according to whether editing is turned on or off.

Symbol	Role
➡	Moves the object to the right.
⇅	Moves the object up or down. Use this symbol if, for example, you wanted to move the `Castle Images` folder to its logical location within the castles topic.
✎	Allows editing of the object to take place.
✕	Deletes the object.
☀	Makes it possible to show or hide the object.
👥	Makes it possible to assign roles to the object.

With editing still turned on, another series of symbols appear on the right-hand side of each topic section as shown in the following screenshot:

The symbols relate to the options available when dealing with the topic sections.

Symbol	Role
☐	Clicking this box ensures that only this topic is visible on the page. It is a useful option for students who have difficulty coping with too much information on a web page or when a teacher wants students to focus on one topic only.
💡	This option makes the particular topic stand out on the page as the current topic. Again, this is a useful signpost for students faced with a large amount of information to negotiate.
👁	This option shows a topic on the page unless the eye is closed in which case students cannot see it. A teacher may be in the process of compiling a topic's contents and may use this symbol to unleash it on to unsuspecting students with a dramatic flourish. It has been known!
↑	Topics can be moved further up the course page. A teacher may decide to change the order in which topics are covered for any number of reasons.
↓	Topics can be moved further down the course page. A topic may need to be moved as a result of an unexpected postponement of a lesson.

Exercise: Using images

Use your uploaded images to create labels with additional information for each topic in the **Y7History** course.

The process for placing each image in the label is identical to the one we used earlier in the chapter. The only difference now concerns the **File picker** menu. You no longer need to select the **Upload a file** option as the folder of images has already been uploaded. Instead, you need to navigate to that folder of images using one of the other options such as **Recent files.** In the next chapter, we shall take a closer look at the files that have been uploaded and where they reside. Our first topic section needs some form of explanation as to what it is. Add the heading 'Introduction' so that it appears in the same way as any other topic summary. Move the Castle Images folder to the **How did castles work?** topic.

- With editing turned off and switching to the role of a student, your course page should resemble the following screenshot:

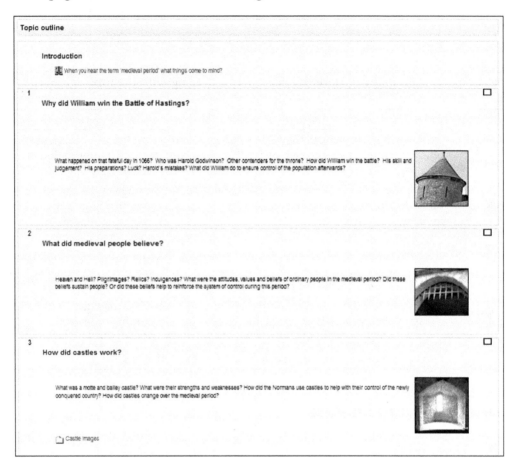

You may feel that there is a fairly large amount of whitespace between the topic summary and the labels we created for the each topic. Is it necessary? How could we remove the whitespace? The workaround would be to remove the contents of the label and insert them in the Topic Summary section using the same HTML Editor as was used when creating the label. Some teachers prefer to keep the course page as tight as possible whilst others appreciate the space provided. As with most activities in Moodle, it is a case of experimenting to determine your preference.

Word clouds

A word cloud is a useful way of drawing students' attention to the vocabulary they will need to use within the course. Any means by which a teacher can get students to use the appropriate terminology in their work should not be ignored and a word cloud is an imaginative way of drawing their attention to the terms they should know about and how they should be spelled.

This point is especially relevant to candidates in external examinations. A good answer stands out if, for example, Josef Goebbels, the Third Reich's chief propagandist, and Tsar Nicholas II are referred to correctly. It indicates a measure of reading around the subject the candidate may have done in order to spell key terms correctly. It points to clear examples of a candidate's own knowledge if the terms are included in the answer but have not appeared in any sources on the paper. And it may tip the balance in a moderator's mind as he or she is deciding between a Level 2 or a Level 3 mark for a particular answer. In this context, a word cloud, positioned judiciously and drawing the students' attention to the key words they need to use and spell with some accuracy, is a pretty useful component. The other point to make is that they are easy and fun to create.

A word cloud can be inserted as an image in a label stretching across the width of the course page. We are going to insert a word cloud in the top section to help students focus on key terms from the medieval period. We are going to start by visiting a website where word clouds can be created. This particular website refers to them as wordles.

1. Log on to `www.wordle.net`.

2. Click **Create**.

3. In the textbox, type as many single words as you can think of connected to the medieval period, separating them with a single space.

For phrases use the tilde ~ between each word such as William~The~Conqueror.

Wordle™   Home   Create   Gallery   Credits   News   Forum   FAQ

Paste in a bunch of text:

```
portcullis invasion trebuchet mangonel siege~tower plague barons villeinsmurder
Black~Death Hastings Thomas~Becket Domesday~Book Edward~the~Confessor
William~the~Conqueror Motte~And~Bailey Stamford~Bridge Harold~Godwinson
Harald~Hardrada Normandy 1066 Contenders Bayeaux~Tapestry housecarls knights
peasants fyrd shield~wall Senlac~Hill witan Wat~Tyler Henry~II John~I Richard~I
```

Go

If you want particular words to appear larger and therefore more significant than others, copy and paste them more than once.

4. Click **Go**.

5. Click **Randomize** to see variations.

6. Choose your favorite version of the wordle.

7. Press the **PrintScreen** button on the keyboard.

8. Paste into your image editor such as GIMP.

9. Crop the wordle and scale it to a height of 180 and width of 600 pixels.

10. Save with a unique filename and a .png extension such as MedievalWordle.png.

Exercise: creating a word cloud

- Insert a **label** in the 'Introduction' section of the **Year 7 History** course.

- Upload your wordle image file to the label.

When it is finished, a student logging in would see a course page resembling the following screenshot:

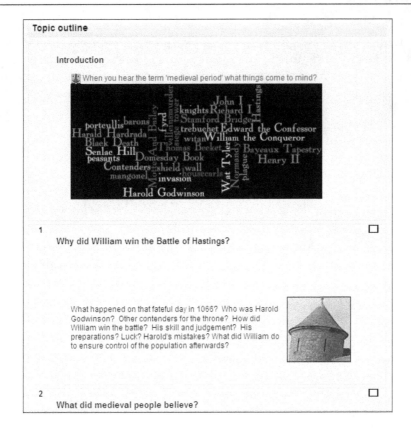

Summary

In this chapter, we have discussed the use of images and labels to create attractive layouts for course pages. Moodle makes it relatively easy to upload and utilize images on a course page. If those images are carefully selected and judiciously placed, then they will enhance the learning process that takes place. A word cloud commands attention on a course page and if it contains a host of key terms that students need to know then the message is being delivered loud and clear every time a student logs in to the course page. Images can be used to reinforce each topic section or they can form part of a story board as you look at the page. It is possible to create small sets of rollovers using the **Appearance** tab when inserting images. It is good practice to prepare the images for use beforehand making sure that they can be found in a named folder and appear quickly on the page. Multiple images can be uploaded to save valuable time. The developers of Moodle have appreciated that an image, selected, edited, and located with care, is worth a thousand words. They have made it straightforward to achieve effective results for the learning process.

In the next chapter, we are going to place useful information in Topic 1 that will help a student with an essay assignment. We are also going to set up a link for all students to submit their essay assignment. We shall create a glossary and see how easy it is to take this a stage further with the creation of a random glossary. This will have the effect of making the course page appear more dynamic and interactive.

3
Adding Interactive Content

We have created courses, added some content and tried to make them look visually appealing. Thus far there has been no real opportunity for interaction between teacher and students. That is a key function of a virtual learning environment. How can Moodle help a teacher to make work available to students? How can it help students to submit work efficiently? What tools does Moodle offer to help in this important area?

In this chapter, we are going to look at how to:

- Upload different types of files to the course for use by students and teachers
- Find the files that have been uploaded so that they can be reused
- Make the files accessible to students
- Create a link so that students can submit a piece of work for marking
- Create a glossary of important historical terms
- Randomly display a different term from the glossary on the course page every time a student logs in to the course

At the end of the chapter, the Year 7 History course will look radically different from how it appears at present. Students will be able to see files that they wish to use and be able to follow a simple sequence of events that sends their work electronically to their teacher. Teachers will be able to follow instructions for placing different types of resources on the course using activities based around the example of medieval history as a useful guide.

Making files accessible to students

Normally, when teaching the year 7 History course, teachers might want to give students an essay question similar to the title of Topic 1, 'Why did William win the Battle of Hastings?'. It may be the first essay that the students have to do for us so we want to be clear about our expectations of them and their piece of work. We can make available to the students a brief document that outlines what we expect of them in terms of their essay style and their own knowledge. The document entitled 'How I will mark the essay' is a typical example. How do we make the document available to students?

In this section, we shall look at how to create a link on the course page within the relevant topic. When the link is clicked, the document appears in a separate window with Moodle still in the background. The following procedure works with any type of document or file that you wish to upload to the course and make available to your students. A link on the course page to a presentation, podcast, or pdf file is created in the same way. Ensure that the file you wish to create a link for has been saved with a recognizable filename. It is then ready to be uploaded to the course. The procedure has similarities to the example in the previous chapter for uploading an image file.

Uploading a file

In this example, we are going to upload the mark scheme we plan to use when marking student essays. The mark scheme is an Open Office document with the `.odt` extension. The logical place for the mark scheme would be in Topic 1 **Why did William win the Battle of Hastings?** We also plan to include a link for students to send their essay directly to their teacher.

1. Open the Yr 7 History course and turn editing on.

2. Locate Topic 1 **Why did William win the Battle of Hastings?**

3. Click on the **Add a resource** drop-down link.

4. Select **File** from the menu.

5. Fill in the details as shown.

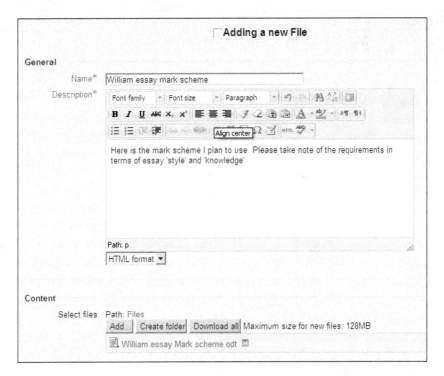

6. Click the **Add** button.

7. Click **Upload a file.**

8. Click the **Browse** button.

9. Navigate to the file you intend to use.

10. Select the file so that it appears in the textbox beside the **Browse** button.

11. Give the file a name to help identify it within the file picker.

12. Click the **Upload this file** button.

13. This action should cause you to be returned to the **Adding a new file** window where we can now concentrate on what students will experience when they click on your link.

In the **Display** setting, you may notice two extra options—**In frame** and **New Window**. I have made these extra items available as Administrator using **Site Administration | Plugins | Activity Modules | File.**

Display option	Outcome
Automatic	Moodle will try to second guess what you want.
Embed	Video and audio files would use this option.
In Frame	The file would appear in one of the frames available on your page.
New window	My preferred option for most cases.
Force download	User is faced with a choice about where to save the file.
Open	File opens directly in full screen.
In pop-up	Similar to New Window but you can specify the size of the pop up whereas new window settings are already fixed.

14. The **New Window** option is our preferred view for students when they click on a link. The window opens automatically in front of the Moodle Course page and students can opt to maximize, minimize, or delete the window, move it, save the file to another location, and so on.

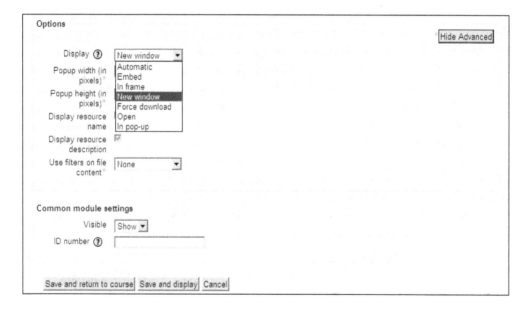

15. Select your preferred display method:

    ° Selecting the **In pop-up** option will activate the Pop-up width and height options.

16. Click **Save and return to course**.

17. The **William essay mark scheme** link should be clearly visible in Topic 1 and when a student clicks on the link it should behave in the way selected in your **Options** choices.

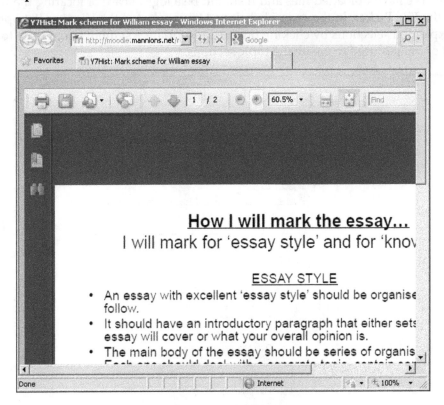

This procedure works for any file that you wish to upload to your course page. Throughout the creation of your courses you will upload a variety of files including word processed documents, spreadsheets, presentations, podcasts, and videos. The procedure will not vary a great deal from the one you have just undertaken.

Where do the files go when they are uploaded?

In previous versions of Moodle, all files went to the same location — the **Files** area in the **Administration** panel — and were not accessible by students unless a teacher made them so. This option is still available to users and appears in the **File picker** as **Legacy Course Files**. It does not appear in the **File Picker** by default however and requires the cooperation of the administrator to make it so.

File Picker and it's options

If you are new to Moodle, then you should investigate the **File Picker** and its various options. We have uploaded files and it should be a logical case of locating them using the **File Picker**. In the example below, I have selected the **View as list** option and expanded selections by clicking on the appropriate **+** symbol to navigate to the folder of images used to create the topic sections.

The files that are uploaded can be found in the **Server files** area and have a logical hierarchy. **Recent files** is self-explanatory and the **Private files** area is a useful addition. Students and teachers can save work in this area and access it at home and school. Previously you had to make separate arrangements for files that you needed to work on in different locations.

Creating a link for students to submit their essays

The next step would be to create a link in the same topic that students could use to submit their essays directly to their teacher. This is a procedure which will also be used many times by teachers when creating courses.

1. Log in to the **Year 7 History** course and turn editing on.

2. Click the **Add an activity** drop-down menu.

3. Select **Upload a single file**.

4. Enter the values shown in the following screenshot:

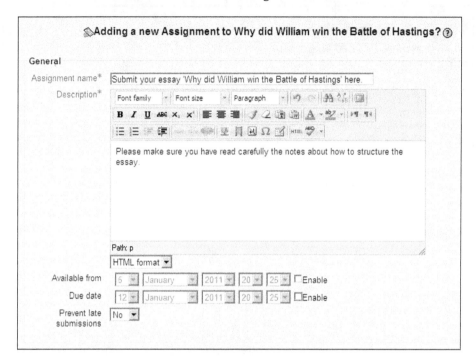

- The **Assignment name** is crucially important. It is the hyperlink that students will click on to submit their essay. It must be unambiguous. 'Submit your work here' is open to many unnecessary complications. Be specific.

- The description can appear alongside the **Assignment** name if you so wish.

- **Available from** and **Date due** have been unchecked but we could select a window when we wanted the work to be submitted by.

- ° We are also prepared to accept work that is late. The screenshot thus shows a relaxed approach to the submission of this piece of work.

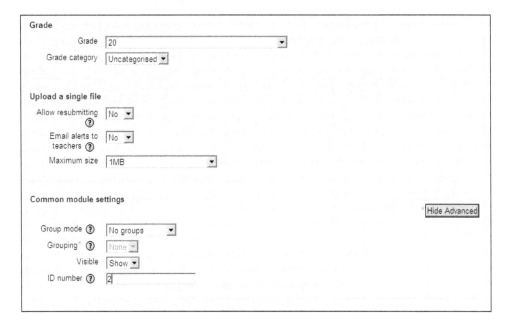

- ° We have elected to mark the essay out of 20 and we shall be looking at marking and the Gradebook in more detail in later chapters.
- ° We could allow students to resubmit their work but we have chosen not to do so.
- ° Similarly, we have chosen not to receive alerts indicating when students have submitted their essay. This is a useful way of chasing up students who have not done so.
- ° We have left the remainder of the settings at their default value. Normally, we would give this task a distinct ID number as it is an important activity that we are going to use for assessment purposes.

5. Click **Save and return to course.**

Submitting an essay

When student FFoyle logs in to the course, the link is clearly visible. To submit the essay, a student would follow this procedure:

1. Click the link beginning '**Submit your ....**'
2. Click the **Upload a file** button.
3. Click the **Choose a file**.
4. Navigate to the saved essay file.
5. Attach it.
6. Click the **Save Changes** button.

   ° Is there a way of the student knowing if they have completed the process properly? Yes, they could quickly check in their **Recent activity** block where there should be a clear indication that this has happened.

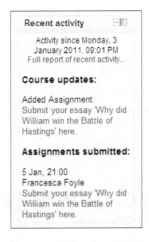

Similarly, how does a teacher know if work has been submitted? We discussed earlier the option to set up e-mail alerts each time an essay is submitted and the **Recent Activity** block shows work that has been submitted. Another way is to log in as a teacher and click on the '**Submit your ...**' link. It should give a clear indication of how many essays have been submitted in the form of a hyperlink.

You are logged in as John Mannion (Logout)

Why did William win the Battle of Hastings? ▶ ...'Why did William win the Battle of Hastings' here.

View 3 submitted assignments

Clicking on the **View submitted assignments** hyperlink gives us our first view of the gradebook.

The essays and their authors are clearly identified. Clicking on Francesca Foyle's essay would open the file directly for a teacher to read and mark. We shall be looking at marking in more detail in later chapters.

A dictionary style glossary

A dictionary style glossary is a useful resource that students can use to look up key terms and find answers to particular questions they may have. A glossary in Moodle can be much more than a word processed document with lots of terms in alphabetical order with explanations for each. Who is responsible for the definitive version of the glossary? Is the glossary in fact, an ever changing and dynamic tool that is being continually updated and refined by other students rather than a static document that some read and others ignore?

A **random glossary** adds another dimension to this because it sits on the page attracting attention to itself and thus enabling students to absorb information and fuels their need to know more about a particular topic, issue, or question. A course about the Cold War could have a random glossary of quotable quotes from the Cuban Missile Crisis.

Setting up a glossary

We are going to set up a glossary that students can use to quickly find information about people, places, and artefacts connected to the medieval period. Initially, it is a glossary that the teacher will populate with information but students also have the necessary permissions to add entries of their own which the teacher can monitor. It will be set up in the top section of the Year 7 History course.

1. Open the Year 7 History course and turn editing on.

2. In the top section, click **Add an activity**.

3. Select **Glossary**.

4. Enter the values as shown in the following screenshot:

The settings I have chosen for the glossary are explained in more detail in the table below:

Item	Description
Name	Provides the hyperlink that students will click on to access the glossary.
Description	A useful reminder of the glossary's purpose.
Entries shown per page	10 is adequate for our needs.
Glossary type	Every course can only have one main glossary but it can have several secondary glossaries. It is possible to export entries from a secondary glossary to the main glossary and this is a useful feature to exploit as the glossary becomes more complex.
Duplicate entries allowed	Set to 'Yes' because there may be more than one entry for the Doomsday Book in the same way that Khruschev would have made more than one entry in the quotable quotes glossary.
Allow comments on entries	Set to 'No' because I do not want my students to comment upon each other's entries. This setting opens up an area that we can come back to look at in subsequent chapters but for now I want to be the sole individual who monitors the glossary entries students might make.
Allow print view	Set to 'Yes'.
Automatically link glossary entries	Administrator needs to have enabled 'glossary auto linking' for this feature to work.
Approved by default	It is set to 'No'. Like many teachers I want to see the work and challenge it before it goes public. The 'Yes' setting is like putting students work on the wall without checking it first.
Display format	Dictionary style is most appropriate for our needs.
Show 'Special' link	Selecting **Yes** enables users to search the glossary using characters such as @ and #.
Show alphabet	Clicking on a letter takes the user to all entries starting with that letter.
Show 'ALL' link	Useful if the user needs to see a list of entries in the glossary.
Edit always	Once entries are agreed upon, I like them to remain fixed so I set the Edit always option to 'No'.

The remaining settings are all connected to the look of the glossary and are worth experimenting upon and selecting your own preferences. Our look of choice for the glossary is the simple dictionary style.

The **Ratings** section allows students to grade each other's entries and again this is a subject we shall return to later. Similarly, in this section, we do not want to target a specific time period when entries must be made. The main glossary is a work in progress and by the end of the course, it will have been a constantly changing and useful resource.

The settings we have chosen enable a teacher to add entries to the glossary. Students can add entries but the teacher will need to have viewed and approved them before they become a visible part of the glossary.

Click **Save and return to course**.

The Glossary of medieval terms now has a link in the 'Introduction' section of our course.

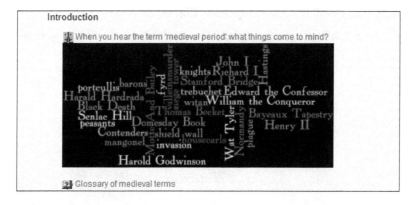

We need to create categories and then add some entries in the glossary.

Categories in the glossary

Efficient use of **categories** makes it easier to search for particular entries and groups of entries. As an example, in the quotable quotes glossary, we would have two categories for the series of quotes and statements. They would be **Pro–American** and **Pro–Russian**. Again, this clearly helps students to compartmentalize the quotes and to learn a selection of them for possible use in an essay.

The entries in our main glossary fall into three categories: people, places, and artefacts. We are going to add three entries to our glossary, one for each category:

- Senlac Hill – a crucial feature of the battlefield at Hastings
- Doomsday Book – William's attempt to survey the country he had just conquered
- Harald Hardrada – Viking contender for the throne in 1066

Creating a category

We are now going to create the category for 'People' and repeat the process for 'Places' and 'Artefacts' before adding an entry under each category.

1. Click the **Glossary of medieval terms**.
2. Click the **Browse by category** tab.
3. Click **Edit categories**.
4. Click **Add category**.
5. In the **Name** field, enter **'People'**.
6. Select **'Yes'** by the **Automatically link this category** dropdown.
7. Click **Save changes**.
8. Repeat steps 4 – 7 for the categories **'Places'** and **'Artefacts'**.
9. Click the **Back** button when you have created the three categories.

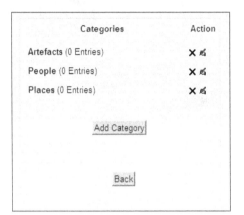

Making a glossary entry

We are now ready to start making entries in our glossary.

1. Click the **Glossary of medieval terms**.
2. Click **Add a new entry**.
3. In **Concept** enter Doomsday Book.
4. In **Description** enter **'William wanted to learn about the country he had just conquered. He commissioned the Book to learn about it. The Book still survives today and is kept in the Public Record Office.'**

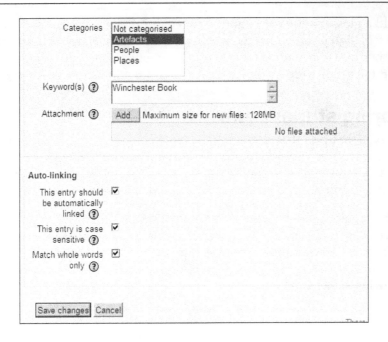

5. Select **Artefacts** in the **category** section.

6. In **Keywords** type **'Winchester Book'**.

7. Tick the **Auto linking** checkboxes.

 Assuming that Autolinking has been enabled by your administrator, this
ensures that when **Winchester Book**, or any keyword added, appears in
the course, it is linked to the glossary term **Domesday Book**.

8. Click **Save changes**.

Exercise: Working with a glossary

Practice what you have just learned by doing the following activities:

- Add glossary entries for:
  - Senlac Hill – a crucial feature of the battlefield at Hastings
    (**Places** category)
  - Harald Hardrada – viking contender for the throne in 1066
    (**People** category)

- Add a new category called 'Norman terms'

- Add a glossary entry for 'motte' – the mound of earth usually around fifteen meters high upon which the keep was built. Early Norman castles were known as Motte and Bailey castles. They took one to two weeks to construct and the locals were usually forced to build the motte.

Monitoring student entries

The glossary is set up so that students can create an entry but it will not be visible until it has the teacher's approval. In the following example, B Foyle and J Foyle create glossary entries. The next time the teacher logs in it becomes clear that entries have been made and need to be made visible in the glossary.

There is clear evidence in the **Recent Activity** block on the course page that glossary entries have been made and they will be grayed out to indicate they are awaiting approval from the teacher. Also, the next time the teacher clicks on the glossary itself the number of entries requiring approval will be shown clearly in a window similar to the following screenshot:

When the teacher clicks on the **Waiting approval** link, the entries become visible and it is easy to approve, reject, or edit them for the glossary using the tick, cross, or edit symbol.

► Introduction ► Glossary of medieval terms ► Waiting approval ► Waiting approval

Waiting approval

Browse the glossary using this index

Special | A | B | C | D | E | F | G | H | I | J | K | L | M | N | O | P | Q | R | S | T | U | V | W | X | Y | Z | ALL
Sort chronologically: By last update | **By creation date** ▲

Harold Godwinson
The only Englishman claiming the throne in 1066. He had the support of the Witan.

(this entry is currently hidden) ✗ 🖉

Witan
A meeting of the most important bishops and earls in England. The support of the Witan was crucial for any claimant tot he throne.

(this entry is currently hidden) ✗ 🖉

Glossary entries challenge the students to synthesize their thoughts and create meaningful explanations to demonstrate their understanding. An interesting and challenging homework could involve allocating a selection of people, places, and artefacts from the medieval world to a class and asking them to conduct some research before creating an entry in the glossary. They will need to classify their entry according to categories you have set up, condense the meaning into a short summary, support it with evidence or an explanation, and include a relevant image. Challenge and extension work comes into this activity through the expert allocation of more difficult terms to the more able students. It is perfectly possible to add images to a glossary. You do it just as we saw in the previous chapter with a label. For the more adventurous students, a glossary entry can also include, for example, web links and audio files.

Altering permissions for the glossary

There are a host of permissions associated with each resource and activity in Moodle and theoretically it is possible for you to turn them on and off, creating opportunities for yourself and students to teach, interact, and learn in a wide variety of ways. It is worth getting to know at least some of the available permissions for each activity and using them to your advantage. Obviously before making any changes it is essenial to do the research to make sure that the correct changes are made. If you recall the point made in the first chapter about the relationship with your administrator changing, it was in reference to these types of changes. Moodle is set up and can be adapted so that teachers and/or students are empowered in their approach to learning and to delivery of learning. The glossary is a rich seam to exploit in this respect and we could examine how to manipulate the way the glossary is set up to achieve such changes.

We could for example, alter the glossary in our course quite dramatically by preventing students from making any entries at all and using it only for reference purposes. This is perfectly acceptable as long as you create other opportunities within your course for students to develop the same skills that they would acquire through the creation of glossary entries. In a later chapter we look at the creation of a database of significant medieval personalities. It could be argued that many of the same skills are duplicated when students research and add their own entry to that database.

A glossary only editable by a teacher

How do you set up a glossary of terms but prevent students from submitting their own entries? You may for example have a list of inspirational or challenging quotes that need to be shown on the page but they do not need to be added to or edited by anyone else.

This approach reverses the default settings for glossaries. It is achieved by consultation with your administrator as it is unlikely that you will have permissions to make these changes on your own. If you do have administrator privileges, then it can be achieved using the following procedure:

1. Log in as administrator to the Year 7 History course.
2. Click **Users**.
3. Click **Permissions**.

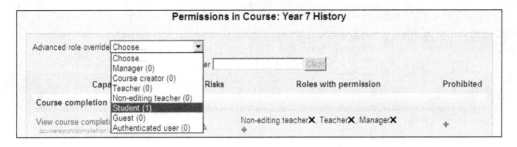

4. Scroll through the permissions list to the **Glossary** section.

5. In the **Advanced Role Override** select **Student**.

6. Select the **Prohibit** radio button for the final entry in the list, **Create new entries**.

7. Click **Save changes.**

The next time a student, B Foyle for example, logs in to the course and clicks on the **Glossary of medieval terms**, the crucial **Add new entry,** which is normally positioned between the **Search** box and the four tabs, is missing.

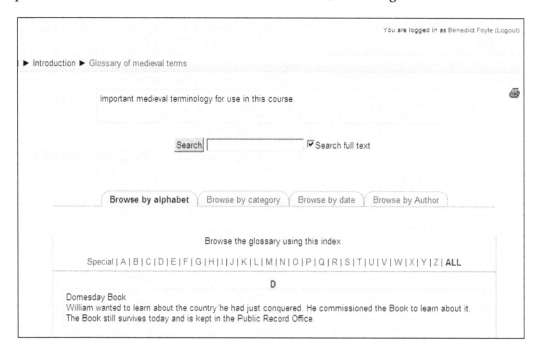

It is possible to add a feature whereby students rate each other's entries and these features can be activated within the settings page for the glossary. We shall look at ratings in more detail later in the book. The glossary highlights key points about the use of Moodle in the teaching of History. It is possible with this module and other modules in Moodle to use a variety of approaches. A teacher who wants complete control of a glossary can set it up to do so. This leads to a rather passive use of the glossary. On the other hand the glossary, like so many other Moodle activities, can involve the whole class in the creation of a resource that they have ownership over because they have collaborated in its creation. The teacher has used his or her expertise to create the parameters and given them the opportunity to develop research skills, to write for a particular audience, and to produce a piece of work that is fit for purpose.

We have not discussed how to add images to a glossary entry because the method is identical to that used in the previous chapter when inserting an image into a label.

Exercise: Further work with glossaries
- Create a glossary entry with an image aligned centrally.

- Create a secondary glossary of medieval monarchs with two categories, Male and Female or a secondary glossary of useful revision tips for your students.

Random Glossary Entry

Having created a glossary, why not get it to do a bit of work for you? A **Random Glossary** gives you the opportunity to show entries on the course page thus displaying students work in the way it was originally intended. It also reminds the students that the glossary is there to be used and many students have commented that it is a way of passively absorbing information through a subtle form of repetition. A random glossary entry from our medieval terms glossary is straightforward to set up.

Create a Random Glossary using a block

The creation of a **Random Glossary** involves our first use of **Blocks** within Moodle. You may have noticed the presence of Blocks on the left- and right-hand side of the main course topics. In the last section about glossaries, we saw the way the **Recent activity** block pointed out the presence of new entries awaiting approval by the teacher. Blocks can be added to the course page and configured to show different types of information. In the next chapter for example, we shall configure a block to show the top five scores by students in a quiz. A **Random Glossary** is a block which displays one entry from the glossary each time a user goes into the course. The other important thing to bear in mind is that they are easy to set up.

1. Log in to the Year 7 History course and turn editing on.
2. Scroll down to the **Block** entitled **Blocks**.

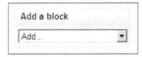

3. Click **Add**.
4. Select **Random Glossary Entry**.

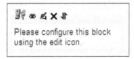

5. Click on the edit symbol in the empty block that has been added to the right-hand pane.

```
                  Configuring a Random glossary entry block

   Block settings

                  Title   Medieval terms
     Take entries from     Glossary of medieval terms ▼
         this glossary
     Days before a new     0
       entry is chosen
    How a new entry is     Random entry      ▼
              chosen
       Show concept        Yes ▼
    (heading) for each
               entry
   You can display links to actions of the glossary this block is associated with. The block will only display
   links to actions which are enabled for that glossary.
      When users can       Add an entry
    add entries to the
    glossary, show a
    link with this text
      When users can
    view the glossary
  but not add entries,
    show a link with
            this text
    When users cannot
       edit or view the
    glossary, show this
    text (without link)
```

The first five fields are self-explanatory.

- ° We have given the block a title.
- ° We have selected the **Glossary of medieval terms** to pick random entries from.
- ° We want a new entry every time the student logs in which might be several times in one day so **Days before** is set to 0.
- ° We want them to see a random entry each time.
- ° We want the student to see the concept given to each entry.

The three remaining fields are interesting. You can add your own text to carry out the command mentioned on the left. The text will appear depending upon the permissions set for your glossary. For example, the text **Add an entry** will not appear if our students cannot add their own entries. However, they can view the glossary so we could edit the second textbox with 'Click here to enter Glossary of medieval terms'. We are not planning to do this because students can already see the glossary on the course page and do not need another hyperlink to it.

The remaining settings relate to where the block is going to be placed on the page and what students will see. We want the entry to be the first thing a student sees in the top right-hand corner of the course page.

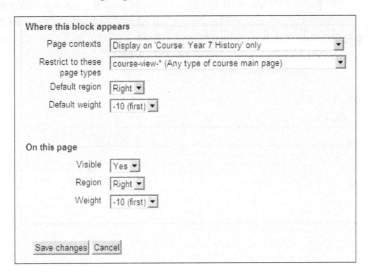

6. Select **-10 (first)** for the **Default weight** setting.
7. Select **-10 (first)** for the **Weight** setting.
8. Click **Save changes**.

When student F Foyle logs in to the course the **Random Glossary** entry will be visible where we have positioned it:

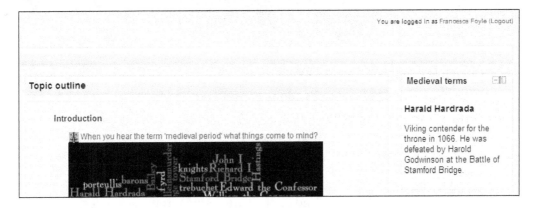

Moving the Random Glossary Entry

The most obvious way to change the position of your block is to turn editing on, reopen the Settings page via the edit symbol, and adjust the selections for **Region** and **Weight.** Moodle offers a more visual way that involves clicking the **Move** arrow and clicking which ever red box position you desire. In the following screenshot, by clicking the empty red box above the **Navigation** block, the **Random Glossary** will appear in the top left-hand corner of the course main page.

1. Turn editing on.

2. Locate the **Medieval terms** Random Glossary block.

3. Click the **Move** arrow.

4. Select the red box where you want to place the **Medieval terms** Random Glossary block.

5. Turn off editing.

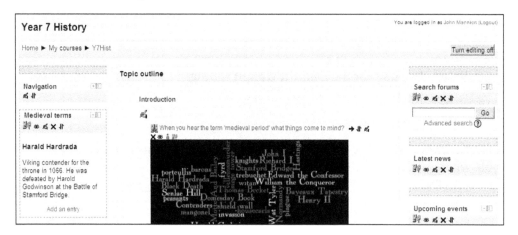

Exercise: A random glossary

- Create a 'Quote of the day' random glossary entry.

- Your starting point will be to create a secondary glossary with some memorable quotes. The 'concept' might have to be a number that is hidden. Why? It cannot be 'author' because you would only be able to select one quote per author which could prove to be a major flaw if you intend to include several quotes by some of the 'big hitters' in History. Format the description carefully so that the author and context are distinct from each other.

- Include a small image of the author in the glossary entry.

- Create a random glossary entry making sure that the **Days before a new entry is chosen** is set to **1** so that it changes each day. A value of 0 would change the quote each time a student logs in and the title 'Quote of the Moment' does not quite have the same ring!

RSS feeds

We will now look at other ways of inserting a 'Quote of the Day' onto the page or another block which updates daily. In the following example, you can see the block entitled 'On This Day In History' which is taken from the BBC website and updates every twenty four hours.

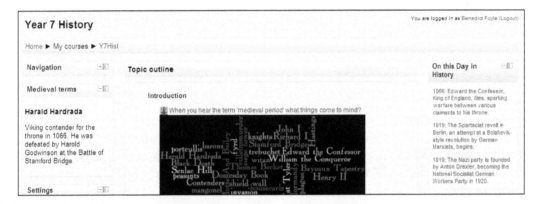

RSS feeds require little work and are a feature that constantly changes and updates without you having to do anything on the course page once it has been set up!

The RSS feeds serve to prompt discussion in class and engage students by reminding them of the relevance of the subject they are studying. When searching for suitable RSS feeds for your site, you need to look out for the relevant symbol on a webpage.

You will need to negotiate with your administrator for permissions to manage RSS feeds on your courses. The administrator needs to turn RSS feeds on throughout the site by going into **Site Administration** and **Advanced features**.

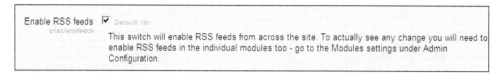

The relevant permissions can be found in the following screenshot when **Teacher** is selected from the drop-down menu at the top of the permissions page:

Moodle provides the news reader so you do not need to worry about that element. Normally, it is a case of following the links that enables you to subscribe to the RSS feed and then copy the link into a specific block on your Moodle course page. The link for the BBC's version of 'On This Day' is http://www.bbc.co.uk/history/otd.xml.

Setting up an RSS feed

You are now ready to add this address to a list of available RSS feeds. Once it is in the list, it can be added to a block and displayed on the page.

1. Log in to the Year 7 History course and turn editing on.
2. Scroll down to the **Block** titled **Add a Block**.
3. Click **Add**.
4. Select **Remote RSS Feeds**.
5. Click on the edit symbol in the empty block that has been added to the pane.

We need to tell Moodle that we want to use the news feed that we have copied.

6. Click the **Add/Edit Feeds** link.

7. Click the **Add a new feed** button.

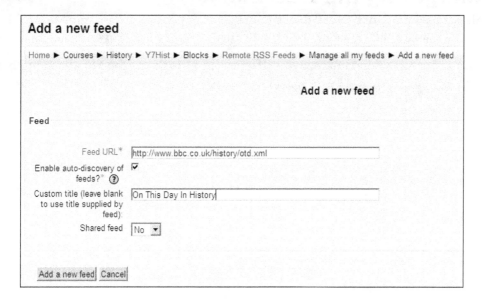

8. Add the details as shown in the screenshot.

9. Click the **Add a new feed** button.

    ° The new feed has been added to the list of available feeds.

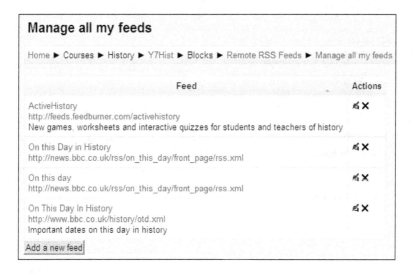

Configuring the RSS block

With our feed now in the available list of feeds, it is possible to configure our RSS block. We can do this by using the Moodle menu bar at the top of our screen.

1. Click the **Y7Hist** link between **History** and **Blocks** on the Moodle menu bar.

2. Locate the **Remote RSS Feed** block in the left-hand pane.

3. Click the **Edit** symbol.

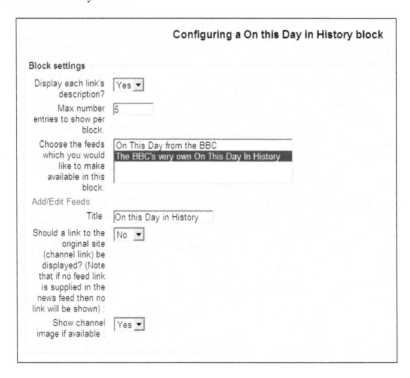

You will see confirmation that the feed has been added. Now, you are ready to make choices about how the block will look when students visit the page. The options we have chosen relate to the amount of space we want the block to take up in the left or right pane.

- ° We have chosen to include the description that accompanies each link.

- ° There will be a maximum of five links in the list.

- ° We have indicated which RSS feed in our collection is to be used by selecting it from the list.

- ° We have entered my preferred title for the block.

- ° We have chosen not to include an extra link to the BBC History site within our block.
- ° We have also decided to include the BBC logo to add a bit of gravitas to the block as it appears. You may want to experiment with these settings to arrive at your preferred look for an RSS feed block.

4. Click **Save changes.**

The remaining settings help to position the block within the course page. Our settings indicate that the block will appear in the top right-hand section of the course page.

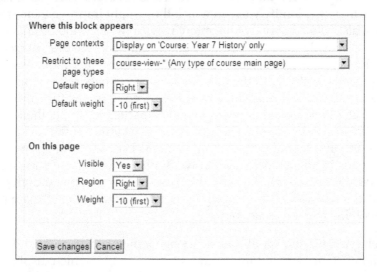

When students log in, they will see a block on the right-hand side that refreshes everyday. In conjunction with the **Random Glossary** entry on the opposite side of the page, you are effectively building up opportunities for students to pursue their own relevant lines of enquiry. You have done this by setting up blocks which require no further attention and will provide a constantly changing diet of links everyday.

The links are wonderful for impromptu discussions for sparking interest and revealing golden nuggets through contributions from the students' own knowledge and experiences.

Summary

In this chapter, we have looked at two essential procedures that course creators will use constantly in the construction of courses—uploading files for students to use and providing links for students to submit their work directly to teachers. A new feature of Moodle, Conditional Activities, enables teachers to stagger the work that students can access depending upon how well they have completed specific tasks. This element of content management is a welcome addition and gives the teacher a measure of control that enhances the learning process for students. They can be required to achieve a particular standard in a task before moving on to the next task. If their essay on reasons for William's victory is weak they can be required to revisit an exercise or carry out a task that helps them to identify ways in which they might improve their grade next time. We have also looked at one of the many ways in which Moodle enables students to collaborate effectively in the construction of relevant and purposeful resources—the glossary. A glossary is an important component in a course and requires planning if it is to be deployed effectively. If the glossary is to be a collaborative work, then the necessary permissions must be set up and entries need to be carefully monitored. If it is a glossary that will be locked down with only a teacher editing it, then the glossary's default settings need to be altered. Glossaries are an example of the constructivist model of learning that Moodle is based on. Students learn and understand more when they have ownership and are actively involved rather than passive participants in the learning process. We also saw how easy it is to insert blocks with random glossary entries and RSS feeds within the course page. This helps to convey the appearance of a constantly evolving and dynamic course.

In the next chapter, we shall continue with this theme of adding valuable content by looking in detail at quizzes and more blocks including one which displays the top five student scores for a particular quiz. Our Moodle course introduces an element of competition to keep everyone on their toes! For those of you who are appalled by such a prospect we will also look at how to turn it off!

4
Quizzes

In this chapter, we will look at different types of quiz questions and creative ways they can be used to enthuse students and challenge them to seek higher standards. We will use a variety of questions and topics to demonstrate the breadth of the quiz tool and just what can be achieved if you go beyond what you might normally offer students. This chapter is not so much about what the quiz can do for you but what you can do with the quiz. Teachers can be creative and inspirational, challenging the brightest while also reinforcing the confidence of the weakest. Investing time in getting to know the quiz feature is one of the most rewarding aspects of a teacher's use of Moodle. Your audience will appreciate it and help to drive future developments.

A Moodle quiz bears no relation to TV game shows. It is instead an opportunity to challenge your students using a variety of question formats. The quiz can be used as an effective lesson starter and equally effective element of a plenary. It can be used to quickly check understanding in class and as an enjoyable homework activity. It can be used seamlessly in examination mode and as a means of challenge and extension. It is of course the individual teachers who use it who make the quiz such a powerful learning tool, and they capitalize on its versatility, which is far too useful to be ignored, particularly in the context of a Moodle course. As teachers get more used to the Moodle quiz they invariably come up with their own uses and part of the fun is making the quiz work for you and your students, revitalising old worksheets, challenging the students to work in a different way. After a brief introduction to the Quiz module, you may well be saying to yourself, "I wonder if I could get it to ...". At that stage, you will have appreciated that the quiz is well worth spending time with and developing rich resources to introduce to your Moodle courses. We shall look at how to:

- Create different types of questions
- Build a variety of quizzes for different purposes
- Construct and manage a question bank effectively
- Offer feedback to students
- Generate automated grading exercises

- Use a block to present a table of results from a particular quiz

Many teachers use it to reproduce electronic versions of their worksheets. This is a perfectly understandable use but is not the only one and ignores much of what this tool can achieve. With quiz creation, feedback from students drives good quiz models forward. Listening to and acting upon feedback is satisfying and leads to long lasting improvements to a teacher's work.

Types of questions

There are a variety of question types available in the quiz. We are going to look at Topic 2 'What did Medieval people believe?' to design some quizzes and using them as a basis, we can explore possibilities including:

- Using the quiz for lesson starters
- Using the quiz to help with the conclusion of a lesson or class activity
- Using the quiz for assessment
- Moving questions between quizzes
- Building the question bank
- Creating results tables
- Using timers

Our quiz questions will centre around a study of life in medieval monasteries which would be covered in Topic 2. Sources will focus on how monks lived their lives, the activities they engaged in during their working day—the trials and tribulations of a medieval monk! We want to set up some questions about the different jobs monks were involved in, including:

- Prior – the man in overall charge, led meetings, and decided punishments
- Chancellor – in charge of money, paperwork, and the library
- Chamberlain – ran the dormitory, looked after the monks' habits (clothes)
- Cellarer – ran the storehouse where food and so on was kept
- Infirmarian – ran the infirmary, looked after any old and sick monks
- Hosteller – ran the guesthouse, looked after any visitors or travelers staying overnight
- Almoner – ran the alms house, gave alms (charity) to the local poor and needy
- Porter – ran the gatehouse, admitted visitors
- Novice – ordinary regular monk

At first glance, it is possible to create several different types of question from this information to reinforce knowledge and understanding or to help with revision:

- A cloze passage where students enter/select the missing words
- A matching exercise where students match the job and description
- A short answer where students type into a textbox the missing word
- True/false outcomes
- Multiple choice questions where one or more answers are possible

Creating a quiz

The first task is to create the equivalent of a cover sheet for the quiz, almost like the front cover of an examination paper that invariably contains the information a candidate needs to read before taking part in the examination. As with an examination paper where you only see the questions after first reviewing the front page, this page must be created before you can start adding the variety of questions. The questions that you create can be used in this quiz and can also be reused in other quizzes.

1. Enter the Year 7 History course and turn on editing.
2. In Topic 2 '**What did medieval people believe?**' click **Add an Activity**.
3. Select **Quiz**.

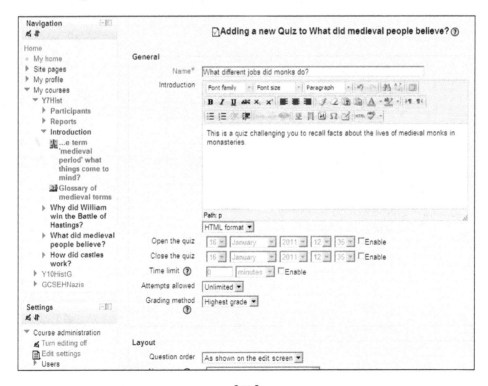

This section of the **Settings** window deals with what students will see when they go into their course and how long the quiz will be available for them to take part.

° The **Name** field is important because this is the text students will click to take part in the quiz.

° The **Introduction** is text they will see having decided to go into the quiz.

° Teachers have the option to rigorously control when and how the quiz is conducted. This is useful if it is to be set as a piece of homework. The teacher can enter the start date and time and the end date and time.

° You can enable the next field and allow students a specific number of minutes to complete the quiz.

° We are going to allow an unlimited number of attempts. We do not plan to use it for any rigorous assessment.

° We plan to record their highest score out of all of their attempts.

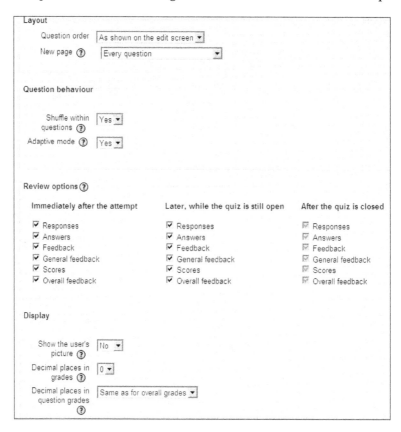

This section of the **Settings** window looks at how the quiz behaves after students have made an attempt.

○ The **Layout** section contains default settings but allows the user to shuffle the order of questions with each attempt and set how many questions will appear on the page. We shall look at the settings in a later, more demanding quiz.

○ We want students to have as many attempts at the quiz as they need and we just want to record their highest score. **Adaptive mode** relates to the penalties imposed on a student who gets all answers correct after five attempts compared to the student who gets 100% at the first attempt. We shall look at **Attempts** and **Grades** in more detail when we look at more comprehensive quizzes.

○ **Review options** for results and feedback will remain at their default settings for this first quiz.

○ In the **Display** section, I want scores to be rounded up to show no decimal places.

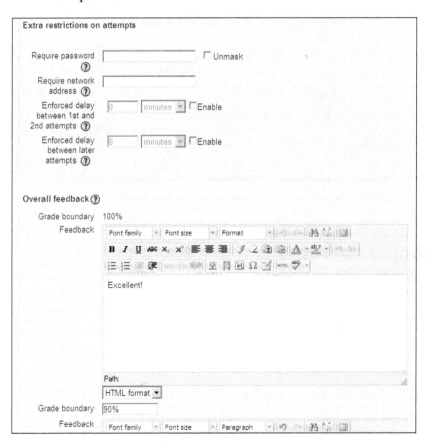

This section of the **Settings** window has further options for student attempts and covers the important area of feedback being provided to students.

- ° With **Extra restrictions on attempts** I do not wish to password protect the quiz. The other options refer to quizzes that need greater scrutiny than I wish to have for this exercise.

- ° In the **Overall feedback** section, I have used single word comments as feedback to students but these can vary depending upon the quiz being undertaken. Each of the five Grade boundaries has access to a full HTML editor and you have the option to add three more. I am using the following values:

Grade boundary	Feedback
100.00%	Excellent!
90.00%	Very good!
80.00%	Good!
70.00%	Satisfactory!
60.00%	Have another go!

- ° **Common module settings** will be more important when we look at groups.

4. Click **Save and return to course**.

- ° Save and display takes you back to the question bank.

The question bank can be seen as a database. As with well-designed databases, it is possible to dip in and retrieve records or in our case, questions to use and reuse as it suits. The question bank becomes more useful if thought is given to the creation of categories and sub-categories to classify questions and make it possible to retrieve them easily.

Creating a category

It is clearly worthwhile to use **categories** to avoid one long list that becomes difficult to navigate. You could quickly create a series of categories that reflect the different topics in the course and then, if you desire, add sub-categories to them. Creating a category is quite straightforward. We shall create a category for the topic 'Why did William win the Battle of Hastings?'

1. Open the Year 7 History course and turn editing on.

2. In the **Settings** block, click **Question bank** to open the question bank.

3. Click **Categories**.

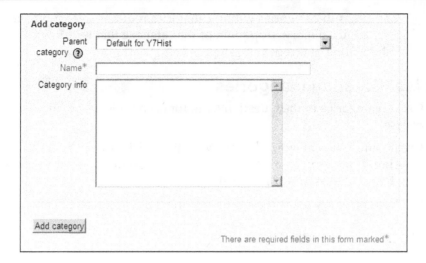

4. Leave the Parent category unchanged because we are adding categories to the Year 7 History course.

5. In the **Name** category, type **Why did William win the Battle of Hastings?**

6. In the **Category Info,** type a brief description of the topic contents or copy the description used in the Topic label on the course page. A good description here helps to locate where particular questions can be found.

7. Click **Add category**.

8. Repeat steps 4–7 for each of the other topics in the course so that the category list begins to take shape:

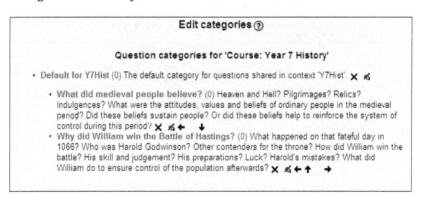

° It is possible to recreate the order in which the topics appear on the course main page by using the **Move** arrows beside each category.

     °   Creating sub-categories within categories requires selection from the Parent category dropdown of the category that requires a sub-heading and repeating steps 5-7.

Exercise: Creating categories

1. Create categories in the Question bank for each topic in the Year 7 History course.

2. Create three sub-categories in the **Why did William win the Battle of Hastings?** category. Name the sub-categories **Contenders for the throne**, **The Battle**, and **William's control**.

     °   Your category list should resemble the following screenshot:

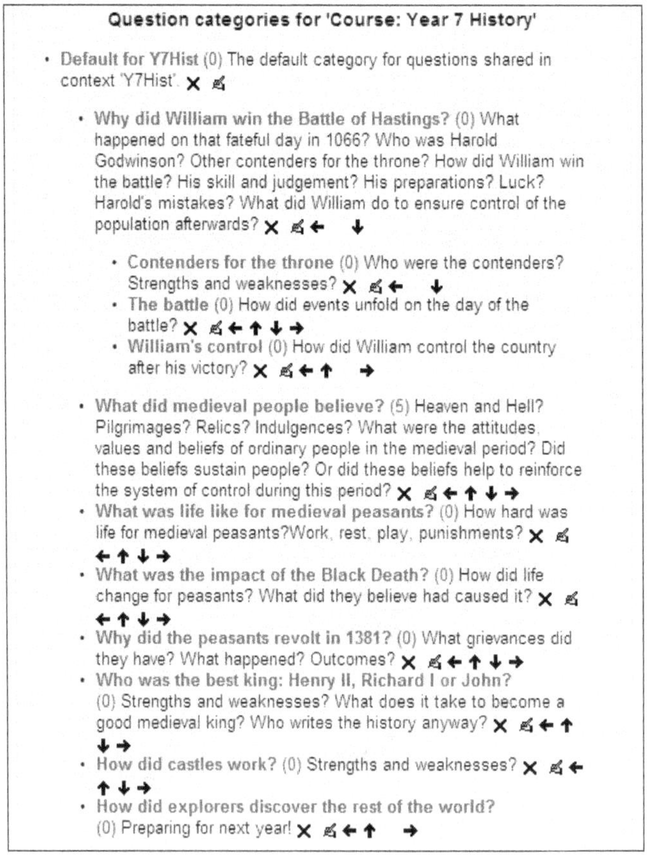

Question categories for 'Course: Year 7 History'

- Default for Y7Hist (0) The default category for questions shared in context 'Y7Hist'. ✗ ✎

  - Why did William win the Battle of Hastings? (0) What happened on that fateful day in 1066? Who was Harold Godwinson? Other contenders for the throne? How did William win the battle? His skill and judgement? His preparations? Luck? Harold's mistakes? What did William do to ensure control of the population afterwards? ✗ ✎ ← ↓

    - Contenders for the throne (0) Who were the contenders? Strengths and weaknesses? ✗ ✎ ← ↓
    - The battle (0) How did events unfold on the day of the battle? ✗ ✎ ← ↑ ↓ →
    - William's control (0) How did William control the country after his victory? ✗ ✎ ← ↑ →

  - What did medieval people believe? (5) Heaven and Hell? Pilgrimages? Relics? Indulgences? What were the attitudes, values and beliefs of ordinary people in the medieval period? Did these beliefs sustain people? Or did these beliefs help to reinforce the system of control during this period? ✗ ✎ ← ↑ ↓ →
  - What was life like for medieval peasants? (0) How hard was life for medieval peasants?Work, rest, play, punishments? ✗ ✎ ← ↑ ↓ →
  - What was the impact of the Black Death? (0) How did life change for peasants? What did they believe had caused it? ✗ ✎ ← ↑ ↓ →
  - Why did the peasants revolt in 1381? (0) What grievances did they have? What happened? Outcomes? ✗ ✎ ← ↑ ↓ →
  - Who was the best king: Henry II, Richard I or John? (0) Strengths and weaknesses? What does it take to become a good medieval king? Who writes the history anyway? ✗ ✎ ← ↑ ↓ →
  - How did castles work? (0) Strengths and weaknesses? ✗ ✎ ← ↑ ↓ →
  - How did explorers discover the rest of the world? (0) Preparing for next year! ✗ ✎ ← ↑ →

This approach does not take long and makes a huge difference when you appreciate what can be achieved with a well-organized question bank. If you have used Exampro software from the site `www.exampro.co.uk`, a database of examination questions, then you will recognize the value of categories. They help you to organize your question bank. It could contain hundreds of questions in an unwieldy list or it could contain categories of questions. Imagine that you want to set up a revision quiz for a particular topic. You can easily drill down to the topic and select relevant questions. Perhaps a question worked well in Topic A and you would like to create a similar one for Topic D. Imagine you want to create an examination based upon the topics covered this year. All of these tasks are achieved easily if you have a well-organized question bank and can identify exact questions. Picture symbols beside each type of question will make this possible. Start from the premise that you will use the quiz module. Indeed, it will become a detailed database over the duration of the course and it will be a time saver and a source of interest and inspiration to students.

We have created a quiz front page and we have created categories. Now, we need to put some questions in the quiz. They are going to be self-marking questions and we are going to start with a matching question.

Creating a matching question

We are going to create a matching exercise involving three positions that medieval monks might have held and short job descriptions. Students will have to match the job with the correct description. We could use the following information in our matching question:

Position	Description
Prior	The man in overall charge, led meetings and decided punishments.
Chancellor	In charge of money, paperwork, and the library.
Hosteller	Ran the guesthouse, looked after any visitors or travelers staying overnight.

The matching question assesses recognition of information rather than recall of information. Achieving success in such a question could encourage students to use this information more willingly in a piece of creative writing. Matching questions work well in History for terms and definitions, events and dates, names and faces, and so on.

1. With matching questions always try to ensure that students do not have to scroll through huge lists to find the correct answer. Ideally, all words and definitions should be visible on the same screen. Open the Year 7 History course and turn editing on.

2. Click the **What different jobs did monks do?** quiz.

3. Click the **Select a Category** dropdown.

4. Select **What did medieval people believe?**

5. Click the **Create a new question** button.

6. In **Choose a question type to add** select **Matching**.

7. Click the **Next** button.

8. Enter the information as shown in the following screenshot:

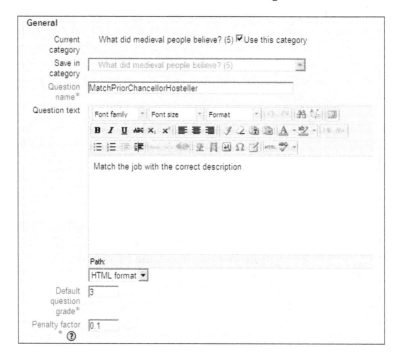

- A descriptive **Question name** will help to identify the question in the Question bank as well as the Matching symbol when it is visible within the Question bank.

- The **Question text** is important as it will walk the reader through the complete process.

- There are three questions and so for **Default question grade** I have entered a value of 3 corresponding to one mark per selection.

If you recall, we placed the quiz in **adaptive** mode and so each time a student gets it wrong in a quiz, a penalty factor kicks in. Thus, a student who gets all of the answers correct at the third attempt does not achieve the same score as the student who scored 100% with the first attempt. A penalty factor of 1 means that the student must get the answer correct at the first attempt to gain credit for it at all. A penalty factor of 0 indicates that the student can have unlimited attempts and still earn full marks for the correct answer.

- ° Ensure that the **Shuffle** box is ticked so that the questions do not appear in exactly the same order each time.

9. Enter the prior's job description in the first Question box and enter **Prior** in the first Answer box.

10. Enter the Chancellor's job description in the second Question box and enter **Chancellor** in the second Answer box.

11. Enter the Hosteller's job description in the third Question box and enter **Hosteller** in the third Answer box.

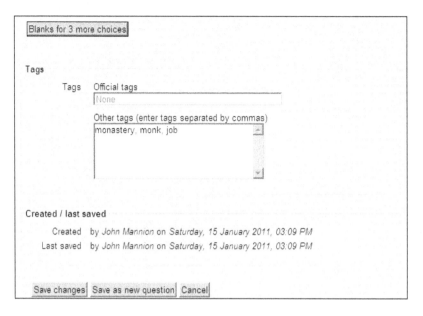

- ○ If you wanted to add more jobs and their descriptions, then use the **Blanks for 3 more choices** button.

- ○ We have looked at the use of tags in the work on glossaries and the same rules apply here.

12. Click **Save changes** to return to the Question bank.

 We could make the question harder for students by decreasing the probability of success through guessing. This is achieved by adding wrong answers accompanied by blank descriptions. The 'distractor' items help to assess recognition rather than a simple recall of information.

Our matching question should be clearly visible in the **Question bank** surrounded by a variety of symbols:

- The double arrow and the checkbox allow us to select the question and to move it to the quiz.

- The matching symbol correctly identifies the question as being of the matching variety.

- The **Edit** symbol allows us to return to the question and modify it if necessary.
- The magnifying glass allows us to **Preview** the question as it would appear to a student.

Other varieties of questions and their related symbol appear in the following screenshot:

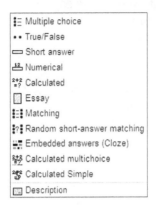

13. Click the **Preview** button now to see the question in action:

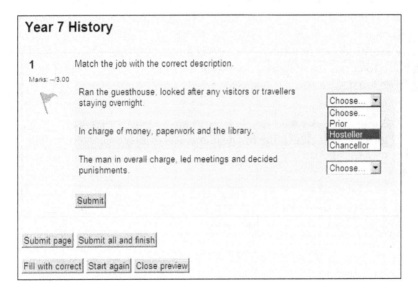

14. Click the **Close preview** button to return to the **Question bank**.

In the next section, we are going to add different types of questions to the question bank category 'What different jobs did monks do?' and you should notice some similarities and differences within the procedures compared with the first example. We shall start with multiple choice questions that include images.

Creating multiple choice questions

Multiple choice questions tend to test for recognition rather than recall. They can test at a fairly superficial level of knowledge or test at a more complex level of comprehension. In History teaching, they can be used effectively with incomplete sentences, statements, or complex scenarios.

 It is important when framing multiple choice questions to ensure that the distractor answers are plausible, similar in length and where possible, contain words such as 'likely', 'rarely', and 'usually'. All of these points make it more difficult for students to discount possible answers without giving each one sufficient thought.

Using some images already stored in the course, we are going to create multiple choice questions for the quiz. Moodle allows you to create simple examples where the reader selects one answer from the list but it also allows more complex questions where the reader has to select more than one answer. Image clues are a useful way of prompting some learners for whom reading the statements is an onerous task. We are going to create one multiple choice question where an image of a cloister has to be correctly identified from a list of locations and a multiple choice question where students have to correctly identify several activities that took place in the cloister by selecting from a list. The former tests knowledge and the latter tests comprehension.

 Some students will right-click on an image and go to **Save picture as** looking for a clue in the image name. Avoid filenames that answer your own questions!!

If creating several multiple choice questions, it would be a good idea to name the questions carefully for identification purposes.

1. Navigate to the Question bank.
2. Select the category **What did medieval people believe?**
3. Click **Create new question**.

4. Select **Multiple choice**.

○ On the **Settings** page, we have chosen a question name that identifies the type of question as a multiple choice with an image and the word 'location'. This will be helpful as the question bank builds up and you find that you want to populate quizzes with a variety of questions perhaps for an assessment of several different topics.

○ We have inserted an image using the file picker.

○ We have awarded one mark for correct identification of the cloister.

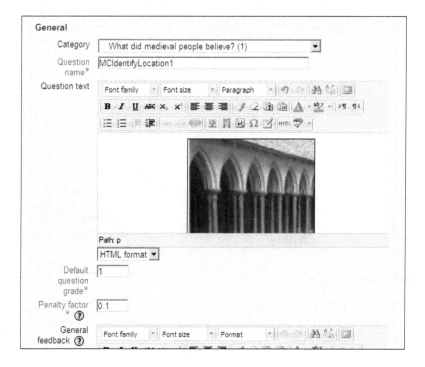

○ **General feedback** is optional and before we enter the list of choices and marks awarded for them, we have to confirm several important choices about the question.

○ Only one answer is correct.

○ The list of options can be shuffled each time the question is used.

○ The answer for cloister must be set to a grade of 100% and the other answers set to a grade of 0 for one mark to be awarded correctly.

○   The remainder of the page contains the familiar feedback settings and the box to enter tags.

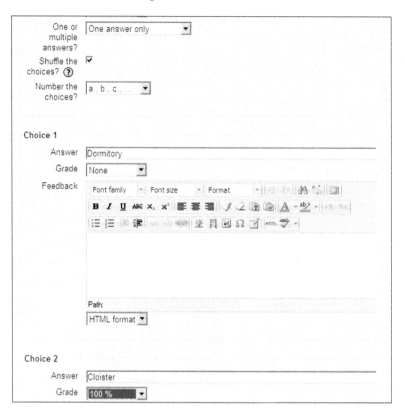

5.   Click **Save changes**.

6.   Preview the question in the Question bank.

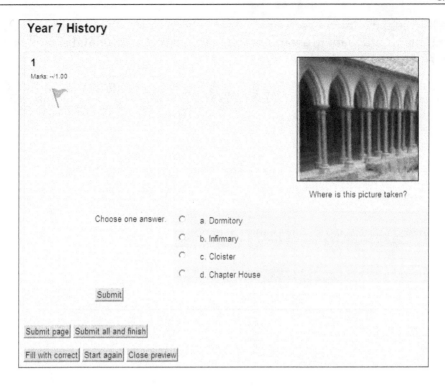

Year 7 History

1

Marks: --/1.00

Where is this picture taken?

Choose one answer.
- ○ a. Dormitory
- ○ b. Infirmary
- ○ c. Cloister
- ○ d. Chapter House

[Submit]

[Submit page] [Submit all and finish]

[Fill with correct] [Start again] [Close preview]

What changes would be necessary for a more difficult multiple choice question where the student had to select more than one answer, as in the following example?

Which statements about the Refectory are correct?

- Monks ate in silence
- Monks were usually permitted to chat quietly while they ate
- A monk was selected to read extracts from the Bible while the monks ate
- The Abbot always ate at the top table

As three of the four statements are correct, we could award three marks for the correct answer. To obtain all three marks the student would need to correctly identify the three correct answers.

Notice how in the following screenshot **Multiple answers allowed** has now been selected. We would want to award 33% for each correct answer and ensure that the question permits more than one correct answer.

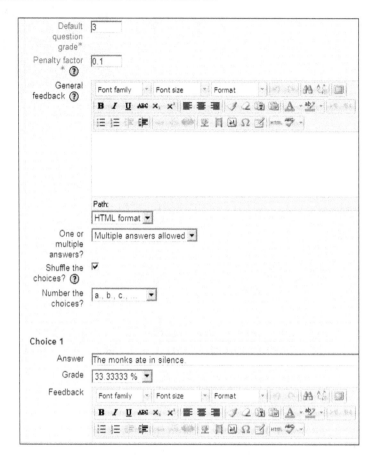

When previewed in the Question bank, there are checkboxes rather than radio buttons because more than one answer must be selected.

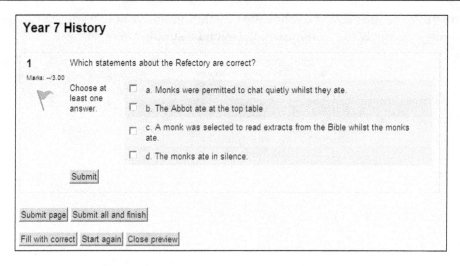

True or false questions

With **True or false** questions, it is important to provide informative feedback to illustrate a point. As there are only two possible answers, it is useful to make the question do a little bit more work for you. We shall use a simple question about the scriptorium to illustrate the point.

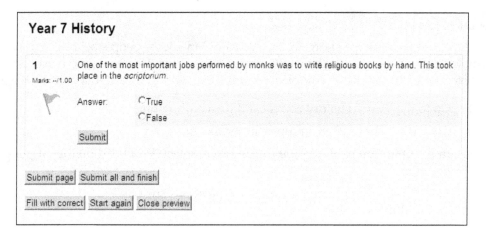

When setting the question, the following illustration shows how feedback can be used quite effectively to extend learning beyond a simple guess:

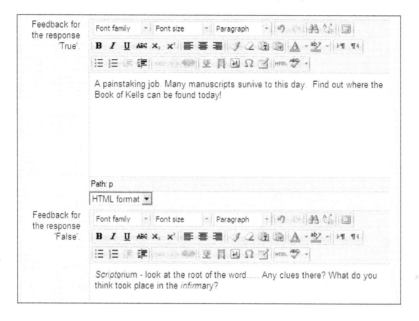

Compiling the quiz

Having created a set of questions for our 'What did medieval people believe?' topic, we now need to create a quiz that students can take part in. We are going to use the questions and when students complete the quiz, they will be awarded a mark out of 20.

1. Go to the Year 7 History course and turn editing on.

2. Click the **'What different jobs did monks do?'**quiz.

3. In the Question bank category dropdown, select **'What did medieval people believe?'**

4. Tick the checkbox beside a variety of questions such as True/false, matching, and multiple choice.

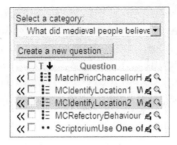

5. Click **Add to Quiz**.

   ° We can now concentrate on the layout of the quiz.

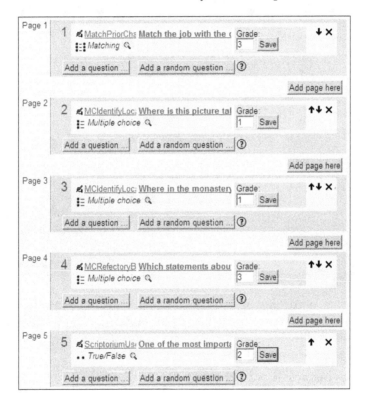

   ° The **Total of grades** figure is the number of marks for each
     question added up. The **Maximum grade** is the figure that the
     scores will be scaled to. In our example, we have increased the
     Grade value of the **True or False** question to 2 so that Total of
     grades and Maximum grade are the same. These are the values
     we intend to use for this quiz. The results will be seen in the
     gradebook in the following chapter.

○ The symbols on the right-hand side enable questions to be moved up and down the order or deleted. We might want both multiple choice questions about the Refectory to appear on page 3 in which case we would use the upwards pointing arrow on page 4 to do this. We would also move the True or False question up to page 4 and delete page 5 using the relevant symbols.

6. Click the **Order and paging** tab.

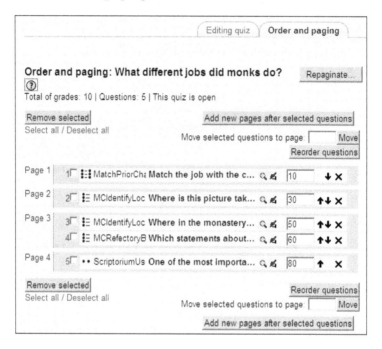

○ Further reordering options are available here. The numbers that are multiples of ten are a clever way of reordering the questions if you decide a change is necessary. Simply revise the numbers as you require and click the **Reorder questions** button.

○ Pages can also be added if you require extra questions to be included.

○ On the left-hand side, questions can be removed from the quiz easily but they will remain in the Question bank. You can view and edit the questions at this stage but once the quiz has been taken by a student, no further editing is possible.

7. Use the Moodle toolbar to return to the Year 7 History course and turn editing off.

The quiz is now ready to be used by students and their results will be sent to the gradebook.

Student View on entering the quiz

When a student logs in and clicks on the quiz link '**What different jobs did monks do?**' a message will appear asking if they wish to attempt the quiz and on clicking it, the quiz will appear with options to submit answers.

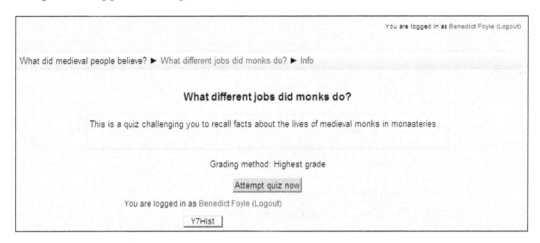

They will need to be told that the **Submit all and finish** button is the same as handing in their work to be marked.

After completing a quiz, students will be given instant access to their results if that is what was selected in the feedback section. They will also be invited to attempt it again if that preference was selected in the quiz settings page.

It is not possible to add a question to a quiz that is already open and students have actually attempted. In order to include the new question, you would need to create an entirely new quiz, using the old questions and adding the extra questions to it. You can hide the old quiz by closing the 'eye' symbol beside it (when editing is turned on!). Students will only be able to attempt quizzes they can actually see.

Displaying a Quiz Results table

Assuming students have attempted the quiz, it is possible to show results in a table of results.

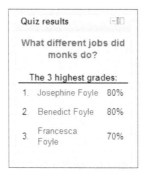

As the teacher, you have control over how many results are shown and what information is displayed. You do need to ensure that such an approach fits in with your school marking policy.

1. Open Year 7 History course and turn editing on.
2. From the **Add a block**, select **Quiz Results**.

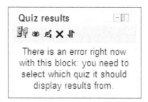

3. Click the edit symbol on the new **Quiz Results** block.

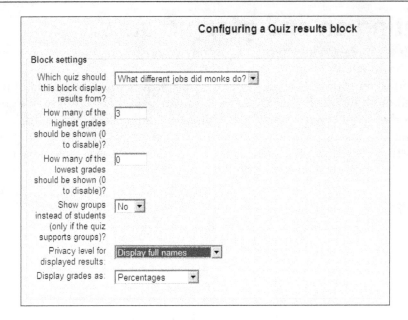

4. In the first textbox, select the quiz whose results you wish to display.

5. In the second box, enter **3** because you want to display the top three quiz performances.

6. Select **Display full names**:

   ° You could choose to display the results anonymously or just use the ID numbers of students

7. Select **Percentages**.

   ° You also have the option to display fractions or absolute numbers.

   ° The remainder of the settings are the same ones as used earlier to position our RSS feed and Glossary blocks on the page and within the course. I shall place the Quiz results on the left-hand side underneath our Glossary of Medieval terms.

8. Click **Save Changes**.

If your students have attempted the quiz, their results will be processed. The table will automatically update when a student completes the quiz.

Students enjoy the added dimension that a bit of competition brings. You can always display results anonymously if your students or senior management are uncomfortable with a league table.

Creating an end of topic quiz

The emphasis in the previous section was on demonstrating how straightforward it is to use the quiz tool. There is no substitute for a teacher's expertise in formulating the questions appropriate to his or her students. A quiz could be an end of topic test to find out how much your students have learned. This could involve creating questions that require written answers. You may want to set a period during which the test must be taken, allow a maximum of two attempts, and be able to differentiate between students who scored well on their first attempt. Students who scored below 60% could be invited to make a second attempt at the test.

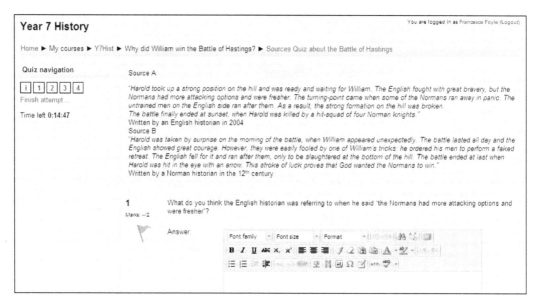

Let us therefore look at a more challenging quiz that requires students to write answers directly into the quiz. The teacher would mark the answers after the quiz has been completed by the students. (We shall look at this manual marking in Moodle in the next chapter). A topic test might contain some text and some questions based on that piece of text. Can we reproduce this in a quiz? The answer is 'yes' and with the added advantage that the quiz can be reused ad infinitum once it has been created, students can access it from home if they miss the lesson and a once tired looking worksheet could be refreshed by color and/or images. Let us base the quiz on the following example:

Source A

"Harold took up a strong position on the hill and was ready and waiting for William. The English fought with great bravery, but the Normans had more attacking options and were fresher. The turning-point came when some of the Normans ran away in panic. The untrained men on the English side ran after them. As a result, the strong formation on the hill was broken.

The battle finally ended at sunset, when Harold was killed by a hit-squad of four Norman knights."

Written by an English historian in 2004

Source B

"Harold was taken by surprise on the morning of the battle, when William appeared unexpectedly. The battle lasted all day and the English showed great courage. However, they were easily fooled by one of William's tricks: he ordered his men to perform a faked retreat. The English fell for it and ran after them, only to be slaughtered at the bottom of the hill. The battle ended at last when Harold was hit in the eye with an arrow. This stroke of luck proves that God wanted the Normans to win."

Written by a Norman historian in the 12th century

1. What do you think the English historian was referring to when he said "the Normans had more attacking options and were fresher"? (2 marks)
2. Find three points on which the two sources agree. (3 marks)
3. Find three points on which the two sources disagree. (3 marks)
4. Can you think of any reasons why these historians have different ideas?
   (4 marks)

Setting up an end of topic quiz

Our starting point is to create a quiz with radically different settings from our first rather genteel quiz.

1. Open the Year 7 History course and turn editing on.
2. Navigate to the '**Why did William win the Battle of Hastings?**' topic.

3. Click **Add an activity** and select **Quiz**.

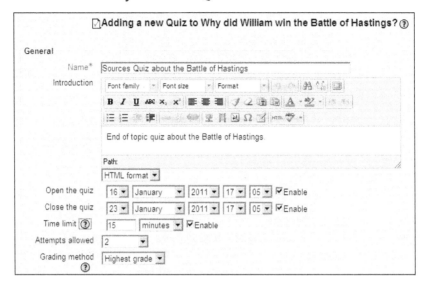

4. Enter a suitable **Name** and **Introduction** for the topic test.
5. Set a start and an end date for the test.
6. Set a time limit of **15** minutes.
7. Set the maximum number of **Attempts allowed** to 2.
8. **Grading method** is set to **Highest grade** because, of the two possible attempts, we want to record the highest one.

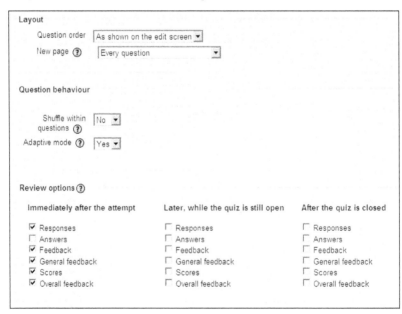

9. Leave **Layout** options at their defaults.

10. Set **Adaptive mode** to **Yes**.

11. Tick the boxes as shown in the **Review options**.

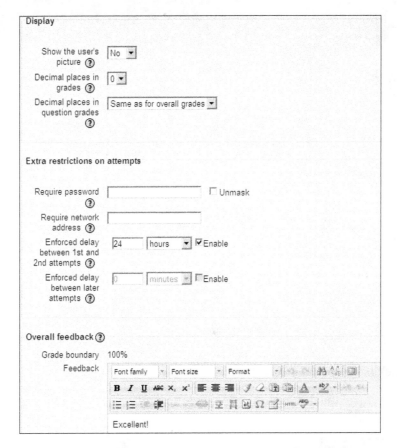

- ○ The first **Display** option allows the teacher to check that the correct student is sitting the test!

- ○ **Extra restrictions on attempts** allows the teacher to set a password or to limit the test to machines within the school's network.

- ○ **Enforced delay between 1st and 2nd attempts** allows us to ensure that students take some time before attempting the quiz again.

○ **Feedback** can be entered that reflects the marking policy.

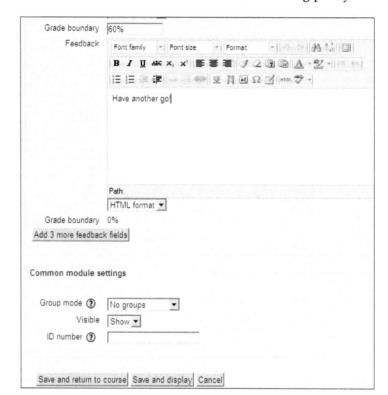

12. Click **Save and return to course**.

We can now create the description and quiz questions.

Description question

When you want to set up a series of questions about a particular piece of text, then you should use the Description option in the Question bank to act as a container for the text. It is not actually a question but it holds those elements that students need to continually refer back to in order to complete the quiz. Our particular test quiz requires a Description and four separate Essay questions. When students attempt the quiz, they will be able to enter their answers directly and when they submit their answers, teachers will be able to read them and apply comments and marks. The results will appear in the gradebook.

1. Enter the Year 7 History course and turn on editing.

2. Navigate to the topic **Why did William win the Battle of Hastings?**

3. Click the new quiz that has been created, **Sources Quiz about the Battle of Hastings**.

4. From the **Select a category** dropdown, choose **The battle**.

5. Click the **Add a new question** button.

6. Select **Description** from the list.

7. Enter the title **Sources A and B**.

8. Enter the text for sources A and B in the **Question text** box.

9. Click **Save changes**.

Essay question

Having created the description that will accompany each question we now need to create the essay questions in the same manner as other types of questions with one or two caveats. Having created and saved the Description question, you should have returned to the Question bank. Make sure **The battle** category is selected.

1. Click the **Add a new question** button.

2. Select **Essay** from the list.

3. Add Question 1 details as shown in the following screenshot:

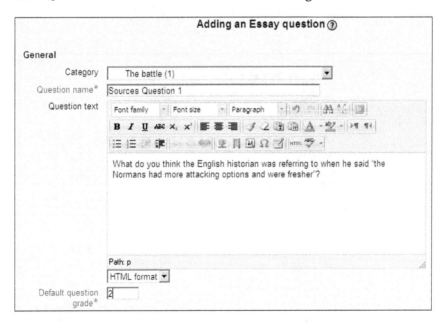

4. Click **Save changes**.

5. Repeat steps 1–4 for the sources questions 2, 3, and 4.

6. The Question bank category **The Battle** should resemble the following screenshot:

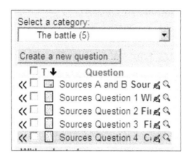

Adding questions to the topic quiz

This procedure is identical to that used with our first quiz. The questions are selected by ticking their checkbox and added to the quiz using the **Add to quiz** button.

Once in the **Editing Quiz** page, all questions need to be placed on Page 1 using the appropriate Move arrows. Pages that are empty need to be deleted. The **Editing Quiz** tab should now look like this:

If you have used the **Order and paging** tab to create the page it should look like this:

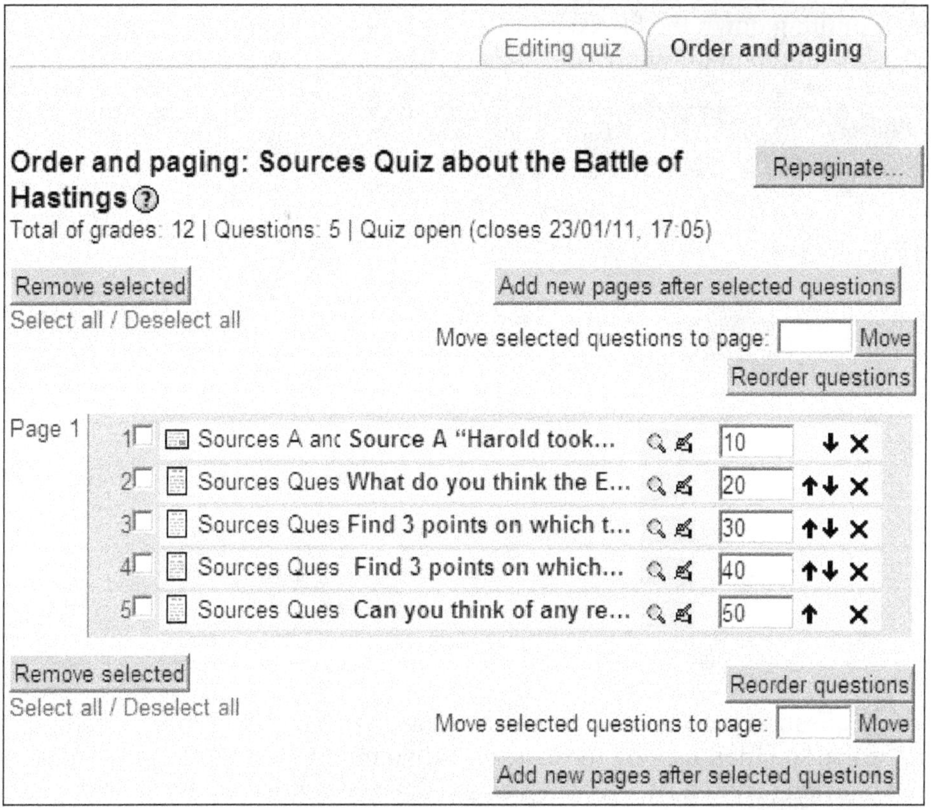

There are variations of layout depending upon your students. You may consider it necessary to have a description above each question so that students do not need to scroll up to the description and back down to the relevant answer box. If this is the case, place each question on a separate page and add a description to each page.

If user FFoyle logs in and selects the quiz, it would appear as in the following screenshot. The marks for each question are visible under the question number. The timer is counting down the fifteen minutes that are available and navigation buttons to access the different questions are also available.

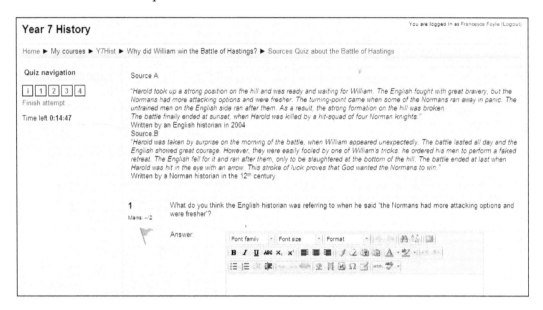

The essay question is different from most of the other question types because it has to be marked manually by the teacher. When might you use the essay question instead of asking students to upload a single file as we did with the question about reasons for William's victory? Any quiz or assessment activity might reasonably be expected to contain an essay-style question as part of it or a short answer question that might consist of one or two sentences. It is preferable for all of the questions to be in the same location for the student.

Although other question types do exist, their creation is identical to the examples we have used. The following table summarizes some points to bear in mind when setting questions using the various question types:

Question type	Issues
≔ Multiple choice	Avoid making it too easy. Make statements plausible and similar length. Use 'always' and 'rarely' to make students ponder the alternatives.
•• True/False	Only two outcomes so a high probability of getting the answer correct. Use feedback to make students work that little bit harder.

Question type	Issues
Short answer	Problem: If the answer is 'Harald' and a student enters 'Harold' how should it be marked? Include all possible misspellings? Only select from a list? Random short answer matching type is an alternative.
Essay	Must be marked individually by teacher. Next chapter.
Matching	Good for definitions, dates, and sequences of events.
Embedded answers (Cloze)	Look good but can be steep learning curve compared to other question types. Useful as comprehension exercises in History.
Description	Not a question but a useful container for image- or text-based sources. Source questions such as 'What do sources A and B agree on? benefit from use of the Description to hold sources A and B.

Cloze passages

Cloze passages are the exception to the rule and require more detailed setting up than any other questions. Many teachers prefer to use Hot Potatoes software, which simplifies the creation of cloze passage questions. It generates a web page that can be included in a course. Moodle however, requires code to be pasted and edited whenever a word has to be entered or selected from a list. In the following example, we can see how it is possible to create a cloze passage from a simple piece of text about the lives of medieval monks.

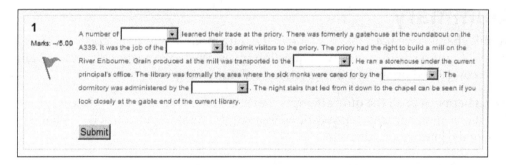

We want to create a multi-choice list for each of the jobs listed in the text so that students have to read the text and select the correct job from that list. This would require a line of code to be inserted where each word should appear.

The question would be created in the usual way, selecting **Embedded answers (Cloze)** from the Question bank's list of question types. The passage of text is entered and where a word has to be selected from the list, we would insert a line of code.

In the first example where the correct answer would be 'novices', the following line of code would need to be inserted:

```
{1:MULTICHOICE:chamberlain~infirmarian~=novices~cellarer~porter}
```

The code for our final answer in the passage where the chamberlain is the monk who looks after the dormitory would be:

```
{1:MULTICHOICE:=chamberlain~infirmarian~novices~cellarer~porter}
```

The rules are that the = sign precedes each correct answer, the ~ separates the different possible answers, and the code is enclosed within a pair of {} brackets.

The result is a neat and tidy solution that challenges students to identify the different jobs within the monastery.

The range of question types available in the Quiz module is extensive and empowers teachers to be creative and innovative with question setting. Revision exercises and short tests can easily be created and indeed a full end of year examination complete with an allocated amount of time could be created with the quiz tool. The settings page for a quiz grants the level of flexibility that you require and it is a case of adapting the quiz to your needs. Planning an effective quiz really is a case of setting down your goals and trying it out. Anything is possible!

Summary

In this chapter, we have taken a look at the quiz module. We have created different types of quizzes with a variety of question types. We have created a question bank for a course and organized the question bank into categories.

What happens to all the quiz attempts that students make and all of the essay questions and short answer questions that require marking by a teacher? That is where the gradebook comes in.

In the next chapter, we shall look in detail at the Gradebook and how it interacts with quizzes and other activities. We shall see how to mark essay questions in quizzes and assignments and how it simulates online marking as used by many examination boards at the moment. We shall see how it simulates the markbook that is central to any teacher's organization and as with any Moodle module, how it can be used to make the teacher's job easier and more productive.

5
The Gradebook

Moodle's **Gradebook** is a hidden gem, a powerful tool given enough time to explore it… The Gradebook enables a teacher to incorporate anything that would normally be done as part of their job into the Moodle experience. If a student submits a piece of work, the Gradebook indicates that it is there ready to be assessed. If a student submits a quiz that involves automated grading, the score and other details are available to view. If a student takes part in a **workshop**, views a **lesson**, (we shall look at lessons and workshops in a later chapter) or takes part in any other Moodle activity, the Gradebook can be used to record each individual's performance. It can be used to generate reports for parent consultations and to assist in writing school reports. Just like a good teacher's markbook, it can be used to inform the teaching as well as record the performance of students. The correct grades for a student find their way into the right place automatically in the Gradebook. A variety of reports can be generated with a few clicks from the information in their Gradebook.

If I were to click on the Gradebook in my Year 7 History course, what would I see? I should be able to see the results of various quiz performances by my three students and I should be able to see, sitting there waiting patiently for me to assess, one essay about why William won the Battle of Hastings from each of my three students.

The Gradebook

Going into the Gradebook via **Settings** and **Grades**, we would see the electronic equivalent of a page from a teacher's markbook showing the names of students and the activities they have been involved in within the course. The Year 7 History course would resemble the following screenshot showing all of the course grades so far:

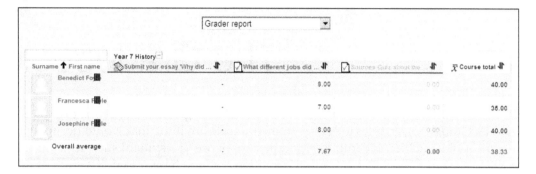

Adjusting Grader Report settings

Most teachers are very prescriptive about the information that goes into their markbook. I, for example, might want to remove the **Overall average row** and set all values to **0** decimal places.

1. Click **Settings**.
2. Click **Grades**.
3. Click **Report preferences**.
4. Click **Grader Report**.
5. Set the **Show column averages** dropdown to **No**.
6. Click **Course grade settings**.
7. In **Grade item settings** click the **Overall decimal points** dropdown.
8. Select **0**.

The Gradebook should now resemble the following screenshot:

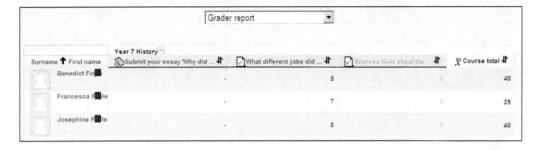

Students are listed in alphabetical order and their marks for the 'What different jobs did monks do?' quiz are detailed.

Clicking the column headed 'What different jobs did monks do?' opens up a view of pupil scores on each question within the quiz. We can see examples of questions where individual students performed well and where they performed poorly.

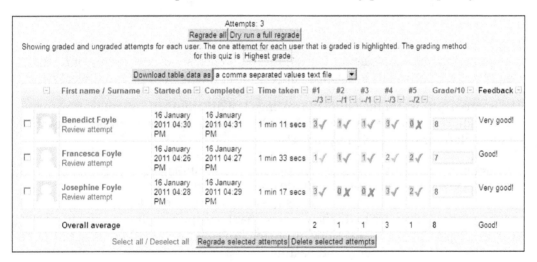

Clicking on the marks awarded to FFoyle for Question 1 opens up a link to that individual student's particular answer, as in the following example:

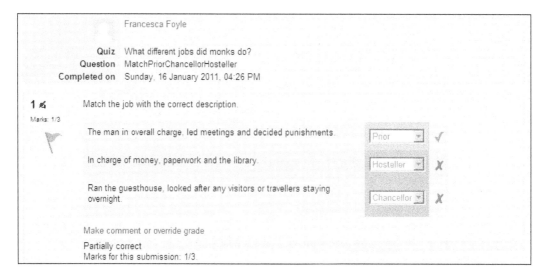

This is useful evidence, informing the teacher about the individual performance of each pupil in microscopic detail. Such information helps with the setting of further tasks that are appropriate and helps address the students' strengths and weaknesses.

The Sources quiz about the Battle of Hastings is a different type of quiz with four answers that can only be assessed by a teacher. How is this done and how does the Gradebook record the teacher's grades?

The method is similar to the online marking many examination boards use with bespoke software. Moderators can grade one particular question or a candidate's whole paper and the grades that are assigned go to the candidate's total. The moderator has little more to do than ensure that they apply their expertise to award the correct grades. Exactly the same approach can be used in the Moodle Gradebook with some additional copying and pasting.

Marking an individual student's response

In this example, we are going to show the marking of BFoyle's answers to Questions 1 to 4.

1. Click the **Grades** link in the **Settings** block.
2. Click the link to the quiz activity **Sources Quiz about the Battle of Hastings.**

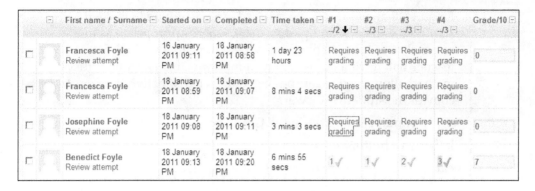

	First name / Surname	Started on	Completed	Time taken	#1 /2 ↓	#2 /3	#3 /3	#4 /3	Grade/10
☐	Francesca Foyle Review attempt	16 January 2011 09:11 PM	18 January 2011 08:58 PM	1 day 23 hours	Requires grading	Requires grading	Requires grading	Requires grading	0
☐	Francesca Foyle Review attempt	18 January 2011 08:59 PM	18 January 2011 09:07 PM	8 mins 4 secs	Requires grading	Requires grading	Requires grading	Requires grading	0
☐	Josephine Foyle Review attempt	18 January 2011 09:08 PM	18 January 2011 09:11 PM	3 mins 3 secs	Requires grading	Requires grading	Requires grading	Requires grading	0
☐	Benedict Foyle Review attempt	18 January 2011 09:13 PM	18 January 2011 09:20 PM	6 mins 55 secs	1 √	1 √	2 √	3 √	7

3. Click the box in the **Grade** column on the row for BFoyle.

4. BFoyle's answers appear on the page.

5. Select the text of BFoyle's answer to Question 1.

6. Copy the text.

7. Click the **Make comment or override grade** link.

8. Paste the answer into the editing window.

9. Mark the question.

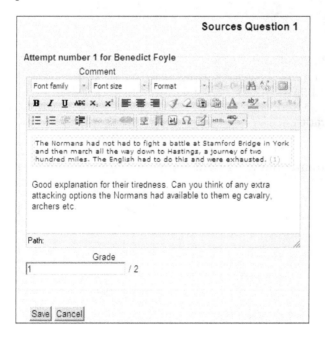

- ○ I tend to change the text color to red, green, or blue to make it stand out and copy and paste a mark where appropriate as in the screenshot or type in comments where they are required. Every teacher will have their own way of marking an answer and this method allows you to reproduce your own distinctive style on a copy of the student's answer.

10. Enter your number of marks in the **Grade** box.

11. Click the **Save** button.

12. Repeat steps 5-11 for each of the remaining questions.

Our marks will appear automatically in the table and will be updated in the grade's window.

- We can choose to mark the same question by different students if we return to the table and select the **Require grading** link under the correct Question number column.

- Students can view their results and see their teacher's marking including how and why marks were awarded.

Marking the same essay question by different students

Three students have submitted their essay on reasons for William's triumph at Hastings. We can mark the essays using exactly the same technique used above. Navigate to the table of submissions by doing the following:

1. Click **Grades**.

2. Click **Grader report**.

3. Click **Submit your ...William essay here**.

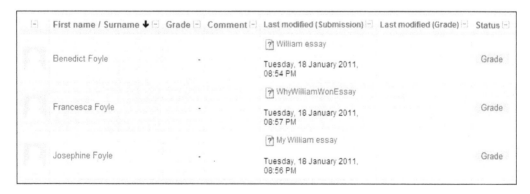

First name / Surname ↓	Grade	Comment	Last modified (Submission)	Last modified (Grade)	Status
Benedict Foyle	-		? William essay Tuesday, 18 January 2011, 08:54 PM		Grade
Francesca Foyle	-		? WhyWilliamWonEssay Tuesday, 18 January 2011, 08:57 PM		Grade
Josephine Foyle	-		? My William essay Tuesday, 18 January 2011, 08:56 PM		Grade

4. By clicking BFoyle's **Grade** link, it is possible to open the essay file, copy it, open the **comment and override marking** editing window, and paste the essay into the window. It can be marked in the same way using steps 9 to 11 mentioned above.

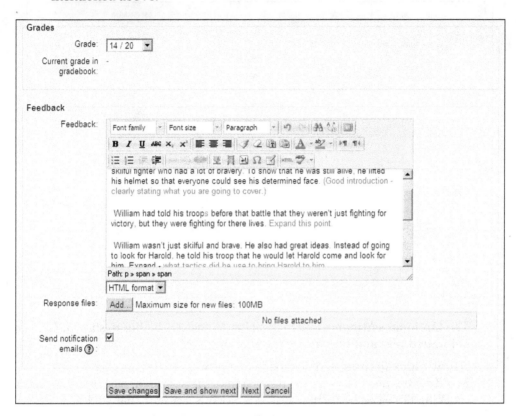

There are several options to consider before completing the assessment of the piece of work.

- The essay grade can be entered using the **Grade** dropdown.
- Teachers have the other option of creating a **Response** file and attaching it for the student to open later.
- Checking the final option sends an e-mail to the students alerting them to the fact that their work has been marked.

The **Save and show next** button takes us to FFoyle's essay, the next essay to be assessed in the Gradebook while also saving the assessment that has just been completed. All assessments and feedback will now be visible in the Gradebook.

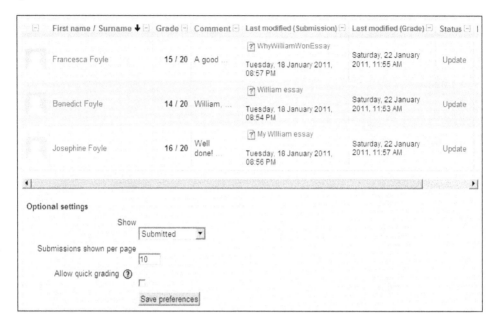

- The **Optional settings** allow the teacher to select whether to show all or just submitted files and the precise number of them.

- **Allow quick grading** enables the above process to be speeded up by avoiding the need to go to the next page to view student assignments. The marking table can be treated as one table. It is a minor change that does not really alter the marking process significantly for essays.

This approach has advantages for the teacher who can see patterns and trends as the assessing gets underway. This should help to inform the feedback that is given to students. If you have considered marking examination scripts, then the procedures do not differ dramatically from the process that Moodle has put into place in the Gradebook. It is rewarding to be able to personalize marking and feedback in this way. It informs the teaching in a way that the traditional markbook cannot do while retaining all of the crucial features of it.

As it stands, the Gradebook seems to treat each activity as of equal value to a final overall mark for the term. The **Course total** calculates a student's total marks and converts it to a percentage.

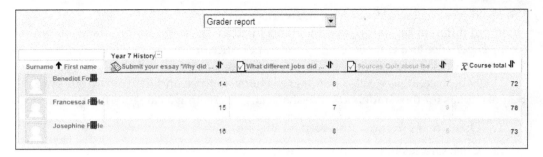

Teachers might want to apply some form of weighting to particular tasks or activities on the course. For example, our William essays carry more importance than the small quizzes that are designed to reinforce understanding of work we have done in class. The essay tests a whole range of skills including knowledge and understanding, essay structure, and so on. and we might want to attach more importance to essay grades in determining how well our students have done. Is it possible to do this? It is and it requires a further change so that we can see how course totals are generated.

Show course calculations

1. Click **Grades**.
2. Click **Course grade settings**.
3. Click **My report preferences**.
4. Click **Grader report**.
5. Set **Show calculations** to **Yes**.

Now, we need to work with **categories** in our Gradebook.

Categories within your course Gradebook

We need to create categories for different tasks within our Gradebook for the Year 7 History course. There are many options for setting categories and it is important to select the correct one for each course. We could create two categories, one for **formative** exercises, and one for **summative** exercises.

Category	Meaning	Example
Formative	Exercises intended to help students develop understanding of the material	What different jobs did monks do?
Summative	Exercises intended for students to demonstrate mastery of the material	Sources quiz Essay ' Why did William win the Battle of Hastings?

We could create categories for **lessons, workshops, blogs, databases,** and so on. We could put different activities or **Grade items** in different categories. It is really down to our experience as a teacher to judge the importance of any activity we ask our students to do. We are going to create categories for Term 1, Term 2, and Term 3. Once they have been created, we can assign grade items to them and then create our own bespoke totals for the Gradebook. We shall start by creating a category for Term 1.

1. Open Year 7 History and turn editing on.
2. Click **Grades** in the **Course Administration** section of the **Settings** block.
3. Select **Categories and items**.
4. Select **Full view**.
5. Click **Add category**.

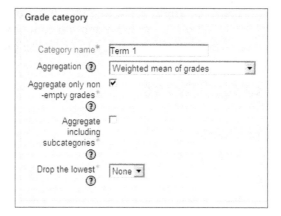

6. Type **Term 1** for the category name.
7. Select **Weighted mean of grades** for **Aggregation**.

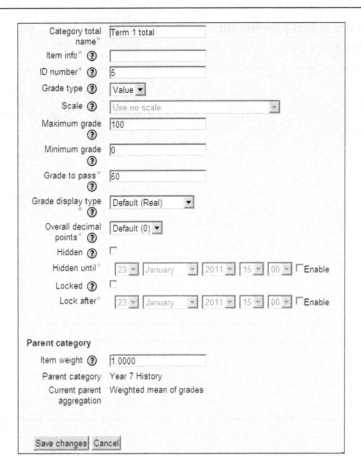

- ° Set the values for the **Category totals** as shown. The **ID number** refers to the number of this **grade item**.

8. For **Grade Category** select **Year 7 History**.

9. Select **Save changes.**

10. Repeat steps 1-7 to create categories for Term 2 and Term 3.

11. Use a unique **ID number** for the activity and enter the maximum and minimum grades.

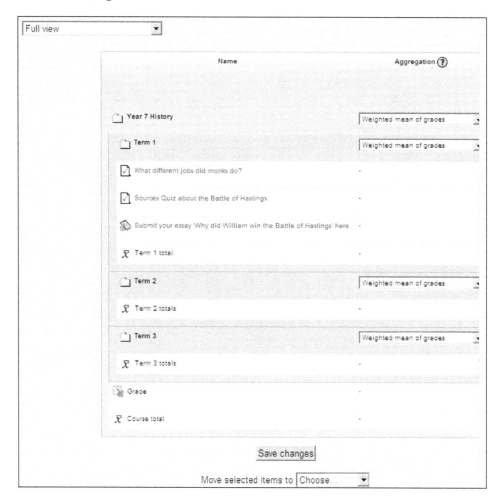

12. The screenshot shows the three categories have been created with the **Category totals** in place. The three different activities or **Grade items** have also been placed in their correct category. How was this done?

Moving Grade items to a category

This organization of the Gradebook is necessary for totals to be generated for different categories. Fortunately, Moodle makes this important process both simple and straightforward. To move **Grade items** into different categories, use the following method:

1. Click **Grades** in the **Course Administraton** section of the **Settings** block.
2. Select **Categories and items**.
3. Select **Full view**.
4. Scroll to the extreme right-hand side of the Gradebook.
5. Click the **Select** checkbox for the essay about reasons for William's success.
6. In the **Move selected items to** dropdown select **Term 1**.
7. Click **Save changes**.
8. Repeat the steps 4-7 to move the sources exercise into the **Term 1** category.
9. Repeat the steps 4-7 to move the quiz exercise into the **Term 1** category.

If we look at the Grader report now we can see some changes with the addition of our categories.

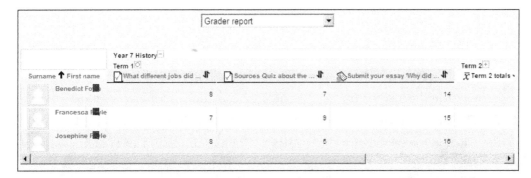

From this point, we can work out Course totals with our own weightings imposed.

Adding extra value to specific grades in your Gradebook

If all of the grade items are in the same category, then it is possible to add extra value to particular grade items to reflect their real value in a student's overall grade for the term. We might regard a summative exercise such as the essay and sources quiz as of more importance than the medieval monks quiz and might want to weight them in the ratio 60%:30%:10%. Here is how to do it with editing turned on in the Year 7 History course:

1. Click **Grades** in the **Course Administraton** section of the **Settings** block.
2. Select **Categories and items**.

3. Select **Full view**.

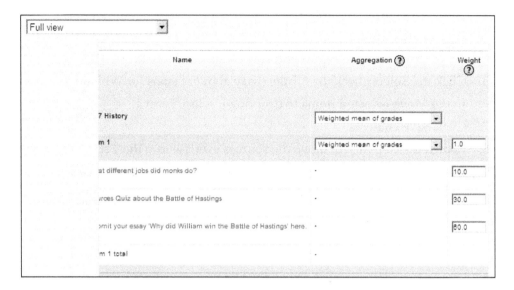

4. Scroll across until you can see the **Weight** column heading.
5. Click in the textbox for the essay submission and enter a value of **60**.
6. Click in the textbox for the sources quiz submission and enter a value of **30**.
7. Click in the textbox for the medieval monks submission and enter a value of **10**.
8. Click **Save changes**.
9. Navigate to **Grader Report** to check that the weightings have taken effect.

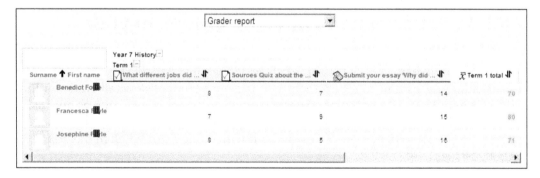

Student FFoyle performed strongly on the two tasks that carried more weight and the overall mark for Term 1 reflects this clearly. Teachers know the value of their various formative and summative exercises. The Gradebook gives them the opportunities to reflect those values in the marks that are attributed to students.

Creating a scale for comment-driven marking of essays

If you recall from earlier in the book, the marking scheme for the essay was comment-driven rather than graded according to marks. The worst outcome a student could obtain would be inadequate for style and inadequate for structure and the best outcome a student could obtain would be excellent for style and excellent for structure. How do we create a scale with these possible outcomes?

1. Click **Scales**.

2. Enter a suitable **Name** for the scale.

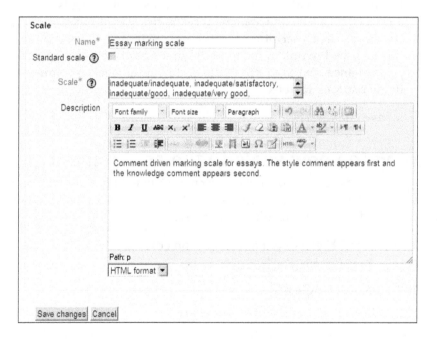

- ° In the **Scale** textbox, we enter the most negative values and separate them with a comma from the next most negative value through to the most positive values. The textbox will look similar to the following and need not take too long to create with some careful copying and pasting: There are five permutations that start with 'inadequate' and five each that start with 'satisfactory', 'good', 'very good' and 'excellent', making a total of twenty-five possible permutations.

  > **inadequate/inadequate, inadequate/satisfactory, inadequate/ good, inadequate/very good, inadequate/excellent, satisfactory/ inadequate, satisfactory/satisfactory, satisfactory/good, satisfactory/ very good, satisfactory/excellent, good/inadequate, good/ satisfactory, good/good, good/very good, good/excellent, very good/ inadequate, very good/satisfactory, very good/good, very good/ very good, very good/excellent, excellent/inadequate, excellent/ satisfactory, excellent/good, excellent/very good, excellent/excellent**

- ° It is important with this more complex scale that students appreciate that the first statement refers to style and the second to structure. The **Description** box becomes extremely important in this respect. It would only be useful in terms of improving their performance next time if teachers added quite focused comments in the marking textbox.

3. Click **Save changes**.

Assigning the new scale to the assignment

The new scale is ready for use. If we were to create a new link in the course for students to submit another essay, perhaps about William's methods for control of the country, we would carry out the following steps:

1. Go into Year 7 History course and turn on editing.
2. In Topic 1 click **Add an activity**.
3. Click **Upload a single file**.
4. Enter values similar to the previous essay.
5. At the **Grade** section, select the new scale from the drop-down list.
6. The new scale appears above the mark for 100 in the drop-down list. You may need to scroll up to the top of the drop-down list to see it. The task can be added to the required **Grade category**.

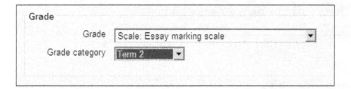

○ When essays come to be marked in the usual way, the newly created scale is available from the **Grade** dropdown instead of the numeric values 1 to 20.

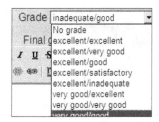

Reports

As with any effective database, the reports that are produced provide crucial information at a glance. If we wanted to prepare for a parents' evening at school, we might want to produce a report overview of grades and general performance with regard to specific tasks. The Gradebook provides us with different options. We can view an individual student's performance or the whole class performance and can add class averages for tasks. This would provide us with enough detail to be able to speak with confidence about the general performance of a student in relation to the rest of the class and to spot possible trends in the course that might need some form of correction in the future.

View student reports onscreen

1. Click **Grades**.
2. Select **User report** from the drop-down box.

3. From **Select all or one user** select **All**.

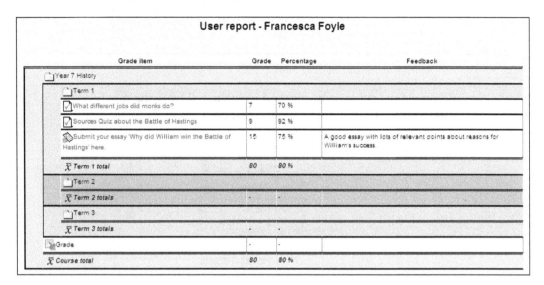

It is possible to print the report in preparation for your parents' evening in the same way you would print any document. Other types of report are available with a few tweaks of the Gradebook. You may, for example, want to talk to an individual student without their necessarily being able to see other students' grades.

Viewing a single student's report onscreen

How do you make only one student's report visible at the correct moment onscreen? You may wish to avoid their being able to see other students' results at the same time as their own.

1. Click **Grades**.
2. Select **User report** from the drop-down box.
3. From **Select all or one user** select a particular student from the list.

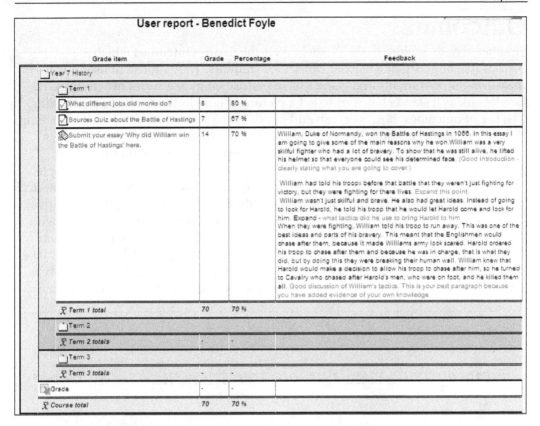

4. The report is now available onscreen or to print out as required. The advantage of using the method of marking that we used earlier (copying and pasting the essay into the editor window to then add comments in a different text color) becomes apparent because the work appears in the report complete with any comments made. Patterns and trends within a particular student's work can be commented upon and targets for future improvements discussed appropriately. All of the information is readily available in this particular report.

Reports can be exported into a spreadsheet if paper copies are required. The Gradebook is a comprehensive tool in the preparation of reports for parents' evenings, chats with students, information for colleagues, and the compilation of term's end reports. The use of ID numbers for grade items and setting up appropriate categories in order to add value to specific grade items are examples of good practice in the use of the Gradebook.

Outcomes

Another area to explore in the Gradebook is the use of **Outcomes** which are measurable targets that a teacher can set for students. They represent useful ways of measuring how students and classes have performed over a series of activities. The Gradebook as it stands helps us to get a picture of how individuals are performing. The use of outcomes, however, can add depth to the picture and inform the teaching that takes place as a result. We are going to add the **Essay marking** scale that we created earlier to the Gradebook. At present, it represents an alternative way of marking the essays if a teacher prefers not to use a grade out of 20. If, for example, the school has a comment-driven marking system and does not encourage numerical marks, then the Essay marking scale as it stands would act as a suitable alternative. By using outcomes, however, the mark out of 20 could be used in conjunction with the Essay marking scale to provide more depth to the Gradebook, showing where student strengths and weaknesses with essay writing might be and helping to make qualified adjustments to class teaching or to the individual student's learning style. Let us look at an example to show how use of outcomes would make a difference.

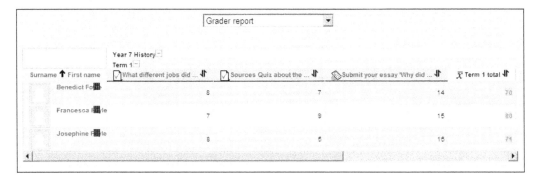

We cannot tell from the Gradebook if BFoyle's essay mark of 14 was obtained through a mark of 7 for essay style and 7 for knowledge or if it came from a different combination—10 and 4, 9 and 5, 8 and 6 and so on. There are at least seven combinations that could result in a grade of 14 without even considering if we wanted to include half marks such as 8.5 and 6.5 and so on. If there was an outcome mark alongside that mark of 14, then at a glance, the teacher could tell a huge amount.

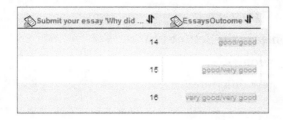

Knowing that the first comment referred to the essay style and the second comment referred to the level of personal knowledge the student had used when writing the essay, the outcomes column shows us that the marks of 14 and 16 were earned with an equal balance of marks in the two sections, but the essay that was marked 15 was slightly weaker in essay style. The intuitive teacher would be able to address the weaknesses by working to improve the student's essay style.

Adding outcomes to the Gradebook

Adding outcomes involves a series of steps. The administrator must first of all enable outcomes. The setting is available from **site administration** and the **Advanced features** link.

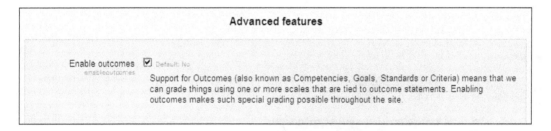

The next stage is to create a scale if one does not already exist. We have already created the Essay marking scale and will be using this in our essay outcomes in addition to the Gradebook.

Creating an outcome

1.   Click **Outcomes** in the **Settings** panel.

2.   Click **Edit Outcomes.**

3.   Click **Add a new outcome.**

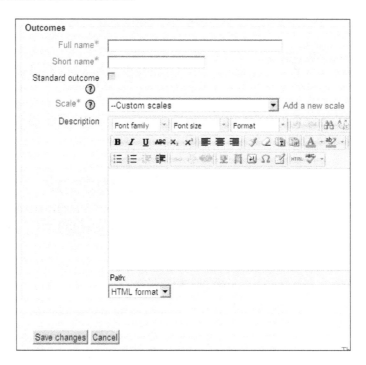

4.   In **Full name** enter **EssaysOutcome.**

5.   In **Short name** enter **EssaysOut.**

6.   In the **Scale** dropdown select **Essay marking scale.**

7.   In **Description** enter **Essay marking scale.**

8.   Click **Save changes.**

The new outcome should now appear in the **Custom Outcomes** table.

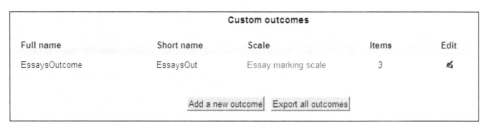

Full name	Short name	Scale	Items	Edit
EssaysOutcome	EssaysOut	Essay marking scale	3	

Assigning an outcome to an activity

We are now ready to assign the outcome we have created to suitable activities. In our example, I would only add it to the essay about reasons for William's victory.

1. Enter the Year 7 History course and turn on editing.
2. Click the edit symbol beside the **Submit your essay 'Why did William win the Battle of Hastings' here** link.
3. Scroll down the **Settings** page to the **Outcomes** section.
4. Check the box beside **EssaysOutcome**.
5. Click **Save changes**.
   - ° In our Gradebook, beside our **Grade** for this activity, there will now also be an outcome which is the Essay marking scale in a drop-down menu.
   - ° It is possible to run an **Outcomes** report to see how students are coping in general.
   - ° It is also possible to run individual user reports and the outcomes appear in the report, helping to inform teachers on progress of students. In the screenshot, we have added the Essay marking scale to the two other activities but have not used the outcomes on them.

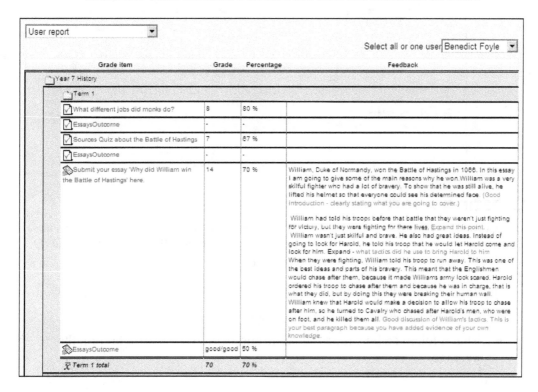

Use of formulae to generate different totals

It is possible to set your own formulae in the Gradebook if you investigate **Full view** with editing turned on and click the calculator icon that appears beside any totals textbox. This really is for teachers who enjoy using spreadsheet formulae and the advantage is that the Gradebook becomes even more versatile — a powerful electronic replica of the paper version that is so important to a teacher's organization.

Assigning ID numbers to grade items

If we are planning to use our own formulae, then it is essential that any grade items we wish to use have unique ID numbers. This is easy to achieve:

1. Click the calculator icon beside the **Course totals** textbox.

2. Enter an ID number for any grade items with an empty textbox.

3. Click **Add ID numbers**.

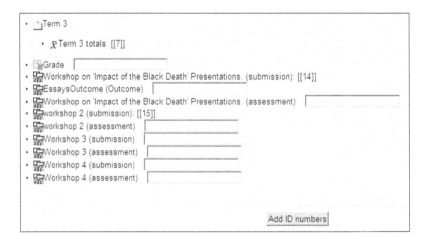

Creating a formula

Our Course total could be based upon the average of the total marks spread over three terms. The total marks for Term 1 has the ID number [[5]], Term 2 has the ID number [[6]], and Term 3 has the ID number [[7]].

Our formula would follow many of the rules for a typical spreadsheet package.

- The formula starts with an equals sign.

- This is followed by a function name and in our case we are finding the average.

- Any Grade items in the formula must be enclosed within their two sets of square brackets.
- Each Grade item needs to be separated by a comma.
- The group of Grade items should be enclosed within curly brackets.

Following these rules allows us to use the formula in the **Calculation** textbox:

1. Click in the **Calculation** textbox.
2. Enter the following formula: =average([[5]],[[6]], [[7]]).
3. Click the **Save changes** button.
4. View the results in the Gradebook by turning editing off and scrolling to the **Course Total** box.

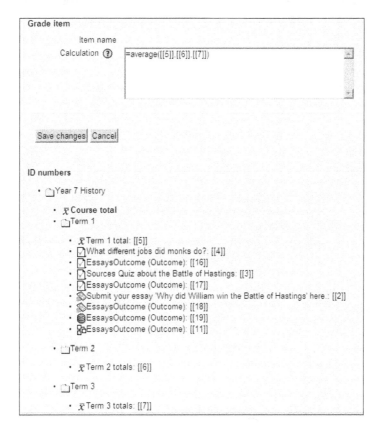

The formula's real value would become apparent when students have completed all of their tasks and activities in the course and accumulated as many marks as possible for them.

Summary

The Gradebook is there to help when completing end of term marking, composing school reports, looking for trends within a student's work, or preparing material for a parent consultation. It can help to spot opportunities for challenge and extension work and to alert a teacher to difficulties a student may be experiencing. A good markbook would do all of this because a teacher has carefully recorded the important details. The Moodle Gradebook reduces the workload significantly because it inserts the data automatically, generates meaningful reports with the click of a mouse, and becomes impossible to ignore in terms of the information about and presentation of student performance.

In the next chapter, we are going to look at more activities that can be recorded within the Gradebook. Specifically, they help to generate collaborative work. We shall look at how students can build up a useful **database** of medieval characters and how they can use a **wiki** to produce a piece of extended collaborative writing about a murder at a medieval monastery.

6
Student Collaboration

In this chapter, we will look at how to set up opportunities for students to collaborate in their learning. Moodle enables students to work together and learn together. A student could for example write their own murder story about a medieval monastery. If however, they are required to work in a group to produce their story, opportunities are opened up to extend their use of historical vocabulary and make the exercise more enjoyable. From the teacher's point of view, the exercise is useful for encouraging students to take responsibility for their work and providing a whole new audience for the finished story. This group approach to creative writing and developing skills of historical research or use of empathy can be achieved through the creative use of wikis. Wikis are just one of the examples that we can look at as we encourage our students to work and learn together. In this chapter, we shall look at how students can be encouraged to:

- Collaborate in producing an extended piece of writing
- Work together on answers to questions that earn the maximum number of marks or points available
- Evaluate each others' work while learning from that actual process
- Contribute records to a database that can be searched, sorted, and interrogated to good effect

Using a poll to stimulate discussion

We shall start by looking at a poll and how one can be used effectively in the classroom.

```
What was the main reason for William's victory? Choose the one reason which you think is
the most important out of the four provided.


  ○ William's skill and bravery
  ◉ William's good luck
  ○ Harold's mistakes
  ○ William's preparations
 ┌──────────────┐
 │ Save my choice│
 └──────────────┘
```

A poll allows the teacher to set a question for which students can then select a response electronically. The poll results are recorded and can be displayed as the poll is being conducted or can be released after the poll has closed. Students have the opportunity to take part in a secret ballot and their responses are not influenced by peers. The poll could be a prelude to a discussion in which poll results are revealed and individuals can argue their case or be persuaded to change their minds. A further poll could take place to see how the discussion has altered opinions. It is a powerful tool when used to get students to focus on the question at hand or to prepare for a lesson. Students could be asked to do some reading and use that as the basis for taking part in a poll.

Setting up a poll

We are going to set up a poll asking students to identify the main reason why William won the Battle of Hastings. Students will be asked to select from one of four reasons:

- William's skill and bravery
- William's good luck
- Harold's mistakes
- William's preparations

We could use the poll prior to the essay the students have to write as a way to get them to see that there is no right and wrong answer and also that the truth probably lies somewhere within a combination of reasons. The poll could form a part of the homework that requires them to do some research for their essay. In this case, the poll is a prelude to a discussion. We could ask the students who voted for one reason to defend an alternative reason in a debate or present the case for an alternative reason. The poll could be used in a number of ways but an effective way would be as a prompt to a discussion. It gives students time to consider the topic to be raised in a forthcoming lesson.

1. Go to the year 7 History course and turn on editing.

2. In Topic 1 'Why did William win the Battle of Hastings?' click on **Add an activity**.

3. Select **Choice.`**

4. In **Choice name** enter **What was the main reason for William's victory at the battle?**

5. In **Choice text**, enter **What was the main reason for William's victory? Choose the one reason which you think is the most important out of the four provided.**

6. In the **Limit** section, we do not want to impose any restrictions on the options that can be selected so this shall remain **disabled.**

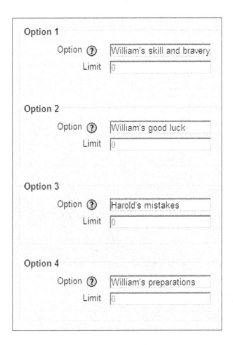

7. In **Option 1**, enter **William's skill and bravery**.

8. Enter the remaining choices in **Option 2, Option 3,** and **Option 4**.

9. We want the voting to take place over **a** week and to close the poll on the morning of the discussion lesson. We will therefore set the opening and closing dates accordingly. Notice that as the teacher you have the power to close the poll at a specific time.

10. We are going to display the options vertically.

11. We do not want students to be influenced by anyone else. This is a secret ballot in every sense so we are opting to **Show results to students only after the choice has closed.**

12. We do want to publish the names and results so in the **Privacy of results,** we have opted to **Publish full results, showing names and their choices.**

13. Give the task a suitable **ID number** and click **Save and return to course.**

14. The poll question will appear in **Topic 1** with a distinctive question mark symbol beside it.

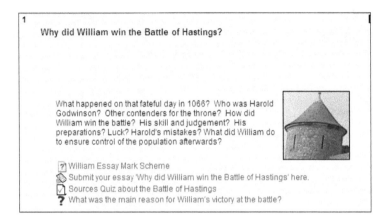

How do students vote?

When students log in to their course they will see the link. Clicking on it will take them straight to their choice.

There, the student selects an option but will not see any results until the choice closes. Once the choice has closed, clicking on the same link will reveal the choices everyone made and hopefully prompt discussion and debate. The teacher can click on the link any time and has the option to **view responses.**

Responses			
William's skill and bravery (2)	William's good luck (1)	Harold's mistakes (0)	William's preparations (0)
☐ Benedict Foyle	☐ Francesca Foyle	The number of user	
☐ Josephine Foyle			

How the individual teacher uses the results is the key (to how effective the activity is). Try to take students out of their comfort zone. If they have selected one reason, why not ask them to present the case for an alternative reason. Create teams in the same way, with each arguing passionately for their selection or make them swap and try to argue equally passionately for an alternative. With an activity like this, try to get students to make connections, spot links between different reasons, and thus understand that events rarely have simple explanations. At the end of the lesson, students could be asked to vote again, electronically or with a show of hands, to see which arguments have prevailed. The poll is a simple and very effective prompt to encourage discussion.

Using a database

A database is another effective way to engage students in the study of medieval history. It is, after all, a collection of related records that can be sorted and searched for information. The Doomsday Book is a form of database which empowered the Normans after the conquest.

The database module in Moodle is not an example of the relational databases that ICT students have to analyze, design, implement, test, and evaluate in their studies. It does not involve creating complex one-to-many relationships between different tables and running queries that produce itemized information. The database in Moodle does however allow straightforward searching and sorting. In the context of asking important questions of History, this is a powerful tool worth mastering and placing in the hands of students.

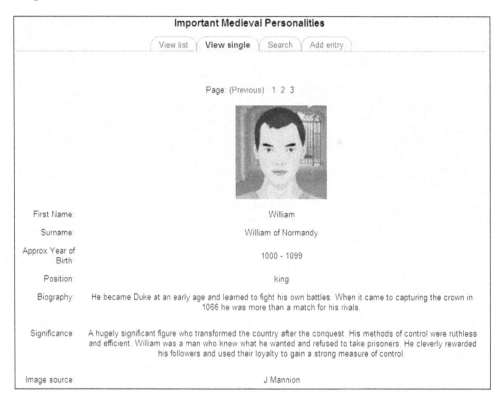

With access to a class bank of computers for a short period of time, it is possible for students to conduct independent research and submit it to a database for others to view instantly. Even without a bank of computers, students can still perform the task and contribute their research as and when they have completed it.

We are going to create a database of important medieval personalities. Each record will be researched independently by a student and after they have found the required fields, their record will be submitted to the database for their peers to view. Each student will have the rights to edit their own record but can only view and not edit the records of other students.

This sharing of information encourages debate and discussion as well as helping students to refine their search skills. The teacher's skill and awareness of students' learning styles should make it possible to allocate appropriate medieval personalities to the right student. The gifted students can of course be stretched by having to investigate the more obscure personalities.

I have used the technique with other courses. In a course about the industrial revolution, an otherwise dry topic was spiced up considerably by allocating a series of inventions and innovations to students and asking them to conduct research with the following question in mind: Why was it the most important invention/ innovation of the Industrial Revolution? The competitive edge takes over as students found themselves arguing passionately about the significance of railways compared to canals or the Spinning Jenny compared to Arkwright's Water Mill.

It is obviously crucial to plan the structure of the database before you start. The more attention paid to planning at this stage, the less likelihood that the structure will have to be altered significantly, thus hindering the actual study of the information. For our medieval personalities database, we want students to take a personality from the period and investigate his or her significance to the period. The fields we want to include in each record are:

- First name – a text field
- Surname – a text field
- Approx DOB – a selection from a list such as 1000–1099, 1100-1199, 1200-1299, and so on
- Position – a selection from a list such as monarch, peasant, political figure, religious figure
- Brief biography – a textarea field that allows lengthier entries
- Image – an image file approx 100 X 100 pixels
- Image source – a text field
- Significance of this medieval personality – another textarea field

It is a good idea to create a data capture form for students to complete before submitting their record to the database.

```
First name: _____        Image source:_____

Surname:    _____        ┌─────────────────────────────┐
                                        │                             │
Approx DOB:_____          │      Image filename         │
                                        │                             │
Position:   _____          │                             │
                                        └─────────────────────────────┘
Biography:




Significance:
```

This gives the student the opportunity to research carefully and remain on task. The teacher can ensure that the correct information is being identified by students before it is entered into the database. The biography field and the significance field allow the student to present the case for the importance of that individual. By using a paper-based approach, you are discouraging those students who feel it is appropriate to copy and paste chunks of text without carefully considering the contents. Each record should be in the student's own words. The data capture form makes this a more realistic possibility. By having to search for and select a relevant image and then crop it so that it appears in the database, students are practising their editing skills and taking responsibility rather than simply copying and pasting from a vague Google search. The image source field also ensures that they give recognition to the source of the image they decide to use. The more time they spend collecting the data accurately the better the quality of the information that the database will return. We can minimize the problem of accurate data entry further by carefully restricting the fields to choices and ensuring that the data that is entered has been carefully considered. The data that is going into our database is going to be validated where possible, thus reducing the risk of what ICT teachers throughout the land refer to as "Garbage in, garbage out!".

Setting up the database

Our Significant Personalities database is going to be added in the top section underneath our Glossary of medieval terms, although it could be placed in any number of other locations on the page.

1. Open the Year 7 History course and turn on editing.

2. From the **Add an activity** menu select **Database.**

3. Enter the values as shown in the following screenshot.

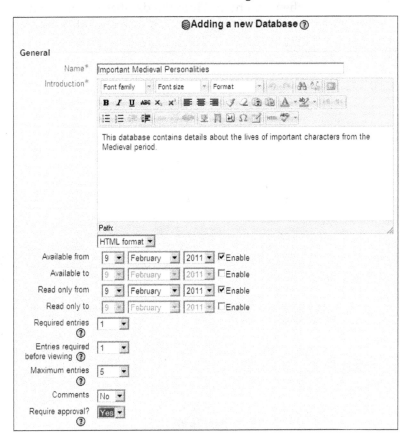

- ° The **Name** field is the text students would click on to enter the database so choose this value carefully. It should be unambiguous.

- ° The introduction provides details about the content of the database. The **Available** and **Read only** values apply to when students can start to enter records and view records within the database.

○ **Required entries** should be set to **1** because we want students to add at least one record before they begin to view the records of others in the class. It is important therefore to set the number of **Entries required before viewing** to **1**. If all students submitted work on five individuals from the Medieval period we would have quite a collection. We are anticipating that students would enter between one and three records. We do not wish them to make comments about other students' records so we will deny them this opportunity. We do wish to monitor the content of the records before they are entered into the database so each entry will require our approval before it can be seen by other students.

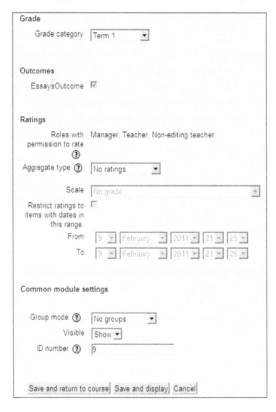

4. Enter the values as shown.

   We want this task to be included in the work for Term 1 and for it to be marked according to the Outcomes we have used for the course. We do not plan to allow rating of the records. We have not set up groups within our course yet but will be doing so shortly when we look at wikis. It is a good idea to add an **id number** to an activity as we have seen, for example, when considering the use of formulae in the Gradebook.

5. Click **Save and return to course.**

Giving students permission to edit entries

The database has been set up and a link will be visible in the course. It is important to change student permissions at this point because the default position is that they cannot edit their records once they have submitted them. This might require some negotiations with your administrator who can access the necessary settings by selecting **Settings | Course administration | Users | Permissions** to get to the following screen:

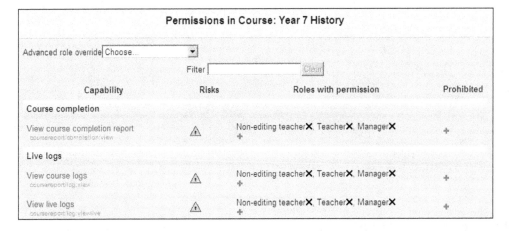

The **Student** option must be selected from the **Advanced role override** drop-down menu. The administrator then needs to scroll down to the **Database** options and **Allow** the options that include **manage, view,** and **write** entries.

This procedure can be done before the database has been set up or it can be done after the fields and templates of the database have been put together. The important point is that it needs to be done before students are ready to add their particular entry into the database.

Adding fields to the database structure

At present, we really only have the link to a database and must now give it a structure. This means adding fields to the database. If we think of a telephone directory, each record has a number of fields including surname, first name, telephone number, postcode and so on. Each field has to be added separately and particular attention has to be paid to the type of data the field needs to contain.

Clicking on the database link in the course page, followed by the **Fields** tab, will reveal the following page:

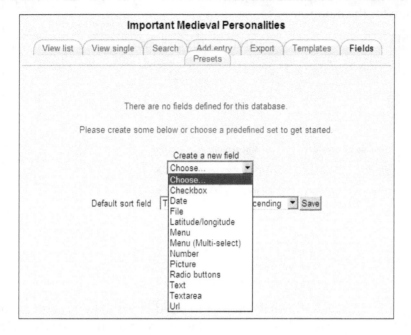

Creating a text field

The first type of field we will create is a short text field for the medieval character's first name.

1. Click the **Create a new field** dropdown.
2. Select **Text** from the available list.
3. In the **Field Name** box enter **First Name**.
4. In the **Field description** box, enter **First name of important medieval personality.**
5. Select **Allow Autolink**.
6. Click the **Add** button.

Exercise: Creating text fields

Create a text field for **Surname** in exactly the same way. The fields will appear in a table design for the database.

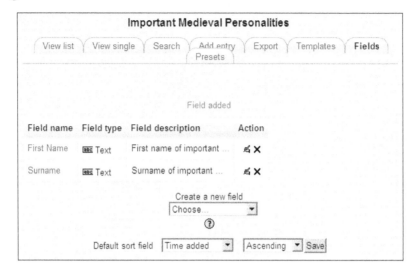

The design of a database allows the author to build in validation rules carefully to minimize data entry errors. The remaining fields, when set up properly, help to reduce the chances of data entry errors.

Creating radio buttons

Radio buttons provide a selection of options and the user can only choose one of them. This would be the option for our approximate **Year of Birth** field. We are going to create a range of options with 100 year gaps. Obviously, you can create as many options as required.

1. Click the **Create a new field** dropdown.

2. Select **Radio buttons**.

3. **Field name** should be **Approx Year of Birth**.

4. **Field description** should be **The approximate period this individual was born.**

5. The **Options (one per line)** box requires that you enter each option on a separate line. Our options are as follows:

   1000 – 1099, 1100 – 1199, 1200 – 1299, 1300 – 1399, 1400 – 1485. This particular task is less about accuracy. You could create more options but equally we want students to appreciate that the medieval period spanned many generations and characters.

6. Click **Add** when finished.

7. You could create a drop-down menu to select from by choosing **Menu** in step 2 rather than radio buttons. This structure prevents students from sorting the records by the **Date of birth** field and this could be a significant disadvantage. It is an important design choice to consider. If you wanted students to be able to sort records by the **Date of birth** field, select the **Number** option.

8. The **Position** field lends itself to a menu, radio button, multi-select or checkbox option. Students need to choose whether their character is a king, queen, knight, baron, political figure, religious figure, peasant, and so on. The checkbox option would accommodate those characters whose role crosses several boundaries. Thomas Becket, for example, would justifiably be a political and religious figure and Watt Tyler would be a peasant and a political figure.

Exercise: Creating checkboxes

1. Create a series of checkboxes for the **Position** field in the database.

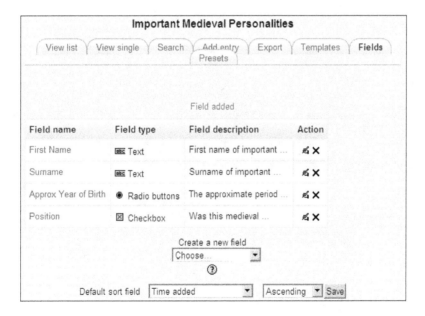

Creating a field for large amounts of text

The **Biography** and **Significance** fields require students to word process their findings into the record and so these fields will contain several lines of text each.

1. Click the **Create a new field** dropdown.

2. Select **Textarea** from the drop-down menu.

3. In **Field name** type **Biography**.

4. In the **Field description** type **key biographical details**.

5. Adjust the number of columns and rows you require for the textbox to **30** and **10** respectively. This would certainly be adequate for the more expansive authors in a group.

6. Click **Add** to add this field to the table structure.

Exercise: Creating a large text field

Add a textarea field for the **Significance** item.

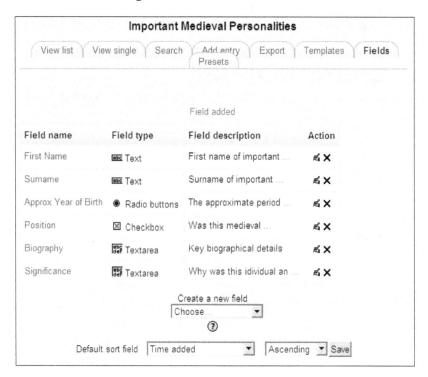

Adding an image field

It is important to have an idea of the size of image you want to display in your records before the database is constructed. When records are viewed as part of a list it is important to reduce the image dimensions compared to the size it could be when each record is viewed separately.

1. Click the **Create a new field** dropdown.
2. Select **Picture** from the drop-down menu.
3. Add the values shown in the following screenshot:

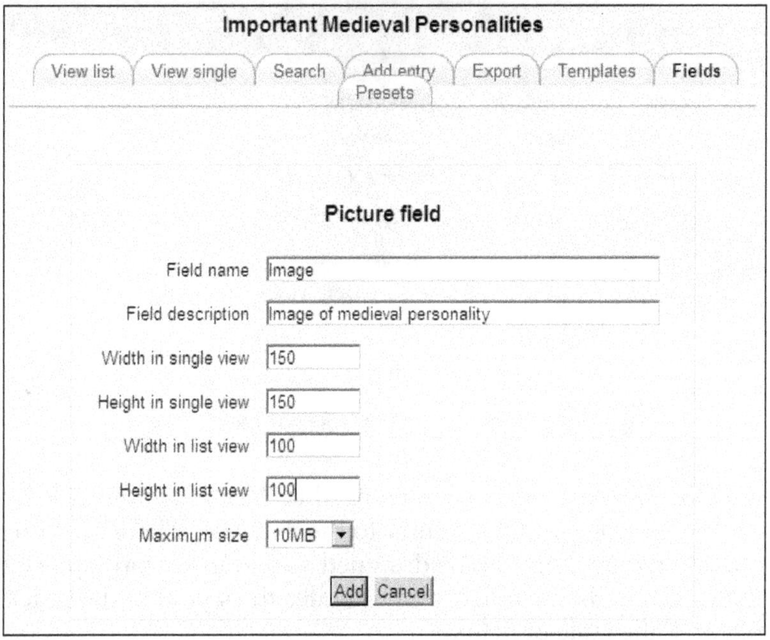

Important Medieval Personalities

| View list | View single | Search | Add entry Presets | Export | Templates | **Fields** |

Picture field

Field name	Image
Field description	Image of medieval personality
Width in single view	150
Height in single view	150
Width in list view	100
Height in list view	100
Maximum size	10MB ▼

Add Cancel

4. Click the **Add** button.

It is of course, good practice to get students to acknowledge the source of their images and we could add another textarea field of approximately three lines so that this can be done properly. It is unacceptable for students to just type the web address of the search engine they have used. The best way to get students to acknowledge that intellectual property is a commodity that has real value is to train them to treat such resources properly.

The database has now been created and the table of fields should look identical to the following screenshot:

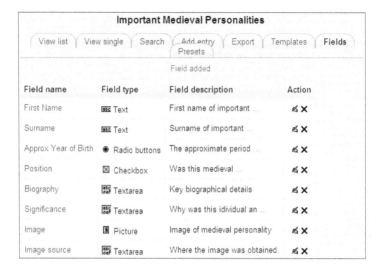

Having created the database table, we now need to design the interface that students are going to use when they add their entry to the database. There are two interfaces, **single** view and **list** view. Both can be designed so that the record appears in the layout that you require. By default, Moodle creates the layout in the order in which the fields appear in the table of fields.

Selecting the **View list** tab displays the records in a list and selecting the **View single** tab displays the records one at a time.

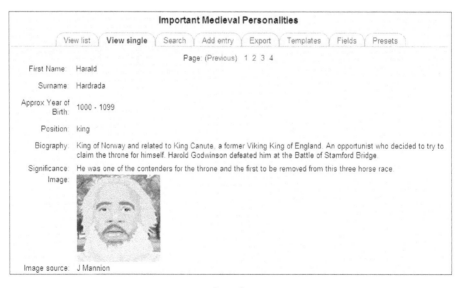

What if we wanted the image to be centered at the top of the record and to remove the superfluous 'image' label beside it? How could we make these changes to the way the records are viewed?

Adjusting the layout of a template

Clicking the template tab opens an HTML table. This table can be tweaked to perform the desired changes.

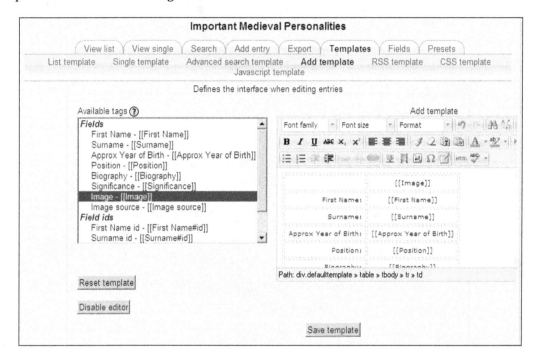

As the screenshot shows, the field labels have a colon and the actual fields themselves are enclosed between two sets of square brackets. All that is required is a small amount of copying and pasting between various cells.

1. Click the **Templates** tab.
2. Navigate across the page to the table containing the list of labels and fields that make up the template.

3. Copy and paste between the cells in the table until you have achieved the following order:

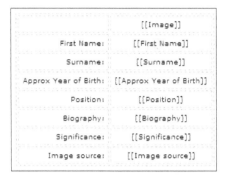

4. Save the template.
5. Click **View single** to see the results of your work.

If further changes are necessary, simply click on the templates tab and return to the table. And how could you remove that superfluous 'Image' label beside the image? Do this by deleting the label and colon from the table, thus leaving the cell in the top left-hand corner blank. In **Single** view, your record should now resemble the following screenshot:

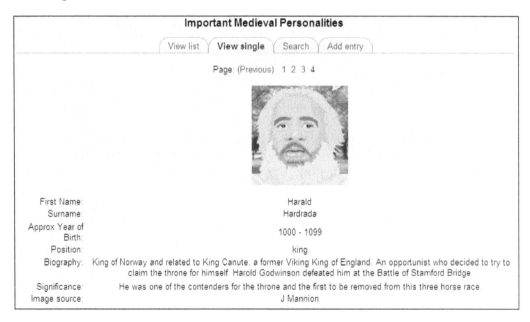

What does a student see in the database?

We have set the database up so that a student cannot see any records until he or she has created and uploaded one first. As a teacher, your job is to ensure that the search skills are producing the right type of information here. The key tab for the student is the one labeled '**Add entry**'. Once the data has been entered and saved via this tab the **View single** and **View list** tabs become available to use. The process of adding an entry should be straightforward if the data capture form has been used properly to collect all of the information required.

Once the entry has been added, nothing can happen until the teacher approves the record. When the teacher logs in he or she will see an enlarged tick beside entries that are awaiting approval and once it has been ticked, a message makes clear that the entry has been approved.

Only the student who created the record or a teacher can edit the entry. The edit symbol appears for the student underneath his or her record.

A well-constructed database with tight data entry guidelines quickly becomes a useful tool for learning. Students can conduct exercises to sort the records by any of the fields and to search for particular fields by entering criteria in the correct textbox. In the example below, the search would result in the record produced by Josephine Foyle appearing on its own.

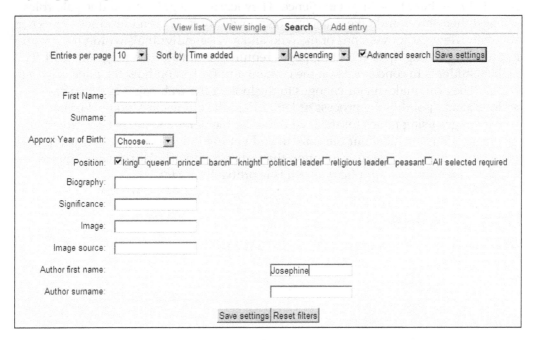

A database is a collection of records and its value is shown when the collection of records work together to produce useful information. It is a valuable exerise to sort the inventions and innovations of the Industrial Revolution chronologically or search the database to decide who was the most important religious leader of the medieval period. Good use of databases within Moodle encourages lively and wholehearted debates. Students will have conducted their own research and equipped themselves with the knowledge and confidence to make an impact on the discussions that arise.

Encouraging collaboration using wikis

Wikis are another tool that get students working together responsibly and collaboratively. Wikis are web pages that can be created and edited on the fly. The only requirement is a computer with an Internet connection. This enables students to work in groups, editing the pages as they see fit. The teacher's role is to set up and manage the groups, giving a clear focus for their web pages. Rather than passively receiving information from the teacher about the causes of the English Civil War, the wiki enables them to carry out their own investigation and present their findings in a way which peers can read, discuss, and debate. The teacher can advise about the direction the wiki should take and sources to look at but the overall presentation of the information is the responsibility of the group members. Students tend to respond positively to this freedom, and to the fact that the teacher's role is that of an informed member of the target audience. They learn to negotiate and delegate roles amongst themselves and take collective responsibility for the end product. A teacher can easily view earlier versions of the wiki and advise individuals within the group accordingly. Setting up and editing pages requires minimal knowledge or effort. This enables students to concentrate on the content and far less on how the page is going to look. They can make major changes to the look of the web pages and that can be done at any point in the process or left as default settings in Moodle. I prefer to prepare pages using tables for the layout and let the default settings take care of how they look. Wikis are all about the content and getting it in place swiftly. If you prefer to spend time on the design of a button that acts as a hyperlink or create complex rollovers, then the raw simplicity of wikis is probably not for you.

Use of wikis

Wikis can be used in a number of different but effective ways during the delivery of History courses.

Year 9 groups (13–14 year olds) at the end of a course on slavery created their own speeches calling for abolition. Each group member was given a different area of the issue to concentrate on from the moral and ethical objections to the economic arguments. The results were quite complex and detailed speeches covered the many different aspects in great depth and everyone in the group felt some ownership of the finished speech. As a task for an individual, it is unlikely many students would have achieved the same level of complexity working on their own. The activity also mirrored the abolition campaigns themselves in that people combined together to make the case for abolition and they eventually won the argument.

Year 10 groups (14–15 year olds) have used wikis to improve examination answers. Wikis have the advantage of making it easy to view earlier versions of the documents and thus it was possible to see how specific changes to answers increased the number of marks earned. It is easy to spot important changes to answers and the resulting increase in marks using a wiki. The **History** tab clearly demonstrates the differences between an answer that is worth five points and an answer worth ten points. The **Compare selected** button also assists with this process of analyzing answers.

In our example, we are going to set our Year 7 group (11–12 year olds) an extended writing activity in groups based around the idea of a murder mystery that takes place in a monastery. The story will build up over a period of weeks and we will guide the groups with specific requirements as to how to develop their story.

The initial task would involve the discovery of a body and the students in the first chapter have to indicate whose body has been found, where and under what circumstances. This task challenges them to explain the significance of key locations such as the cloister or the herb garden.

A later task would involve identifying a number of characters at the monastery who could be potential suspects. This gives students the opportunity to create characters with typical jobs found in the medieval monastery and demonstrate understanding of how monks spent their day.

Another task might be to include a reference to the Black Death within the story. Students therefore have to discuss how to incorporate details they have learned such as symptoms of the disease or fantastic explanations that arose for the causes of the disease.

The denouement would involve the discovery of the culprit and the revelation of details surrounding the murder.

Each task will require students to add details to the story from the knowledge they have gathered about life in the medieval period. Throughout the task, the emphasis would be upon using the students' knowledge about the medieval period and monasteries in particular, to inform the writing. Each member of the group can go in to the wiki, locate the chapter concerned and contribute their part of the story. The editing can be traced through the **History** tab and the final version of the story is the result of extended collaboration from within the group.

The Wiki module allows participants to work together on web pages to add, expand, and change the content. Pages can easily be added containing ideas to develop, images to stimulate discussion, or diagrams for a similar purpose. Old versions are never deleted and can be restored. The wiki is a powerful tool for writing extended pieces collaboratively.

There are some important considerations to make during the initial setting up of the wikis. These are to do with the composition of your groups. It is important to take control of the composition of groups, setting out clear expectations of roles and responsibilities within the groups. Each group will have a separate character and identity. One group might be comfortable with making changes to each others' work while this might be a fairly combustible issue in other groups. Perhaps a rule that group members can add material but not change another member's work would solve the problem. Equally, another group might assign a full editor's role to one member. This has the danger that one person might end up doing all of the work! The success of the wiki is dependent upon careful consideration of how your students interact with each other and making choices that are best suited to their strengths and weaknesses.

Creating groups

Students that are enrolled on a particular course can be placed in groups for purposes of working together on a wiki. Their work cannot be seen by members of other groups until it is published by the group. We are going to create a group called Murder Mystery 1 and it will comprise of Benedict Foyle and Josephine Foyle. Groups can be as large or as small as you wish.

1. Open the Year 7 History course and turn on editing.
2. In the **Settings** panel, select **Course Administration**.
3. Select **Users**.
4. Select **Groups**.
5. Click **Create Group**.
6. In the **Group Name** field type **Murder Mystery 1**.
7. Click **Save changes**.

Allocating students to a group

1. Once the group has been set up, students need to be placed within a particular group.

2. Select **Murder mystery 1** in the left-hand pane.

3. Click **Add/remove users** under the right-hand pane.

4. Select **Benedict Foyle.**

5. Hold down the *Control* key and select **Josephine Foyle**.

6. Click the **Add** button.

7. Click the **Back to groups** button.

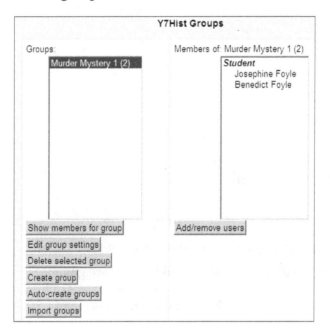

° The number 2 in brackets indicates that two students have been allocated to the Murder Mystery 1 group and the right-hand pane provides their names.

Creating a wiki for a group

The group Murder Mystery 1 have decided to call their story 'Blood on the Riverbank' and so I shall create a wiki with this title in the topic 'What did medieval people believe?'

1. Open the Year 7 History course and turn on editing.

2. In Topic 2 click the **Add an activity** dropdown.

3. Select **wiki**.

4. Beside **Wiki Name** enter **Blood on the Riverbank**.

5. Beside **Wiki description** enter **A murder mystery at the monastery**.

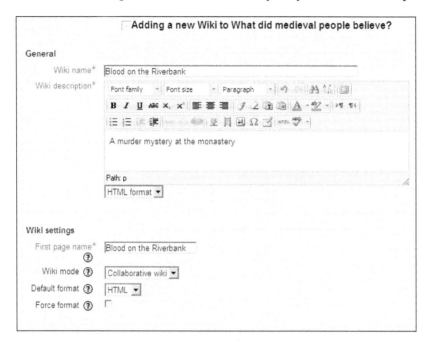

6. Beside **Wiki Mode,** select **Collaborative wiki**.

    °   There are different types of wiki but we are going to stay with the HTML format. As you become more aware of the features of wikis, you may find that you want to experiment with the various formats.

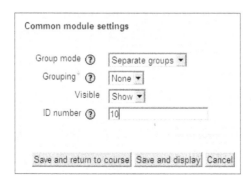

7. Beside **Group mode** select **Separate groups**.

   ° The group mode has been set to **Separate Groups** because we want the groups to work in isolation from each other and only reveal their work when it is completed.

8. Give the task an **ID number** of **10** for the Gradebook.

9. Save the changes.

Assigning roles to the wiki

Having successfully created the group and the wiki, we now need to assign roles to students and teachers so that they can make use of the 'Blood on the Riverbank' wiki. This procedure in effect ties the group to the wiki for the purposes of writing content on the web pages that are created. If a student has not been assigned the role within the wiki then they will not be able to contribute or collaborate in the exercise. We are going to assign student roles to BFoyle and JFoyle, and a teacher role to JMannion.

1. Open the Year 7 History course and turn on editing.

2. In Topic 2, click on the **Assign roles** icon beside the **Blood on the Riverbank** wiki.

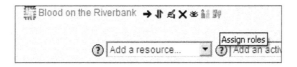

3. Click on the **Student** link.

4. Select BFoyle from the right-hand pane and holding down the *Ctrl* key, select JFoyle from the same pane.

5. Click the **Add** button.

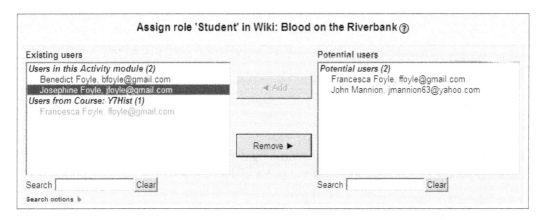

6. Click **Back to list of roles** to see the names have been added to the correct role.

7. Repeat steps 3 to 5 in order to add a teacher to the teacher role.

   ° The teacher role is crucial to the success of the wiki. Although students have a wide degree of freedom when it comes to the content of the wiki, a teacher is responsible for checking the progress of the work. This can be done in a variety of ways. The **History** tab can be used to check who is actually contributing within the group and the **Comments** tab can be used to offer information and advice for the development of the piece of work.

How groups start to use their wiki

When JFoyle enters the course and clicks on the **Blood on the Riverbank** link she can immediately start to create chapter titles on the first page. Enclosing each link within double square brackets ensures that she is effectively creating web pages.

If JFoyle saves the changes and selects the **View** tab, the hyperlinks created are clearly visible.

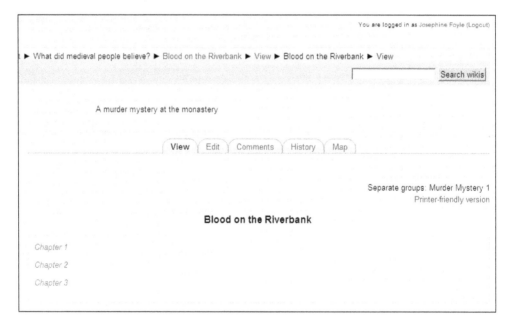

Thus, when BFoyle logs in for the first time he can click on the **Edit** tab and change the **Chapter One** hyperlink to **Chapter One – Discovery** and begin describing the discovery of the body on the chapter one page by clicking the hyperlink followed by the **Edit** tab. It is that easy!

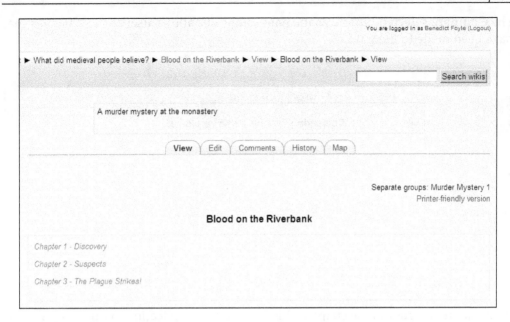

Each time the page is edited and saved, details are logged in the History section and clicking on that tab reveals the information.

The **Compare selected** button, as the name suggests, allows users to see changes that have been made to the wiki.

As mentioned earlier in the chapter, this has a useful application, particularly if students are trying to compare examination answers to understand where extra marks can be obtained.

Groups tend to take ownership of their wikis and respond enthusiastically to the creative freedom it offers them. It is thus a powerful tool that gets students collaborating and learning together, sharing good practice and enjoying the opportunity to work practically under their own initiative.

Summary

In this chapter, we have seen how there are tools available within Moodle which enable students to work closely on tasks that enhance their understanding of historical questions and issues. They can use the wiki to collaborate on extended pieces of writing or their examination technique. There is scope to link wiki pages to outside repositories such as Flickr. This would enable images of medieval monasteries to accompany the stories and enhance the experience for both authors and readers. Students can use the database to help formulate responses to complex questions by searching for and sorting information that has been efficiently compiled.

In the next chapter, we will see how the lesson module can be used to capture a teacher's expertise and reinforce learning. We shall also see how students can be encouraged to develop a variety of useful skills through their use of Moodle's blog facility.

7
Lessons and Blogs

Moodle's **blog** is the tool that showcases a student's interest in the subject of History and captures the date of important experiences in their development as real students of the discipline. It can be a marvellous tool for encouraging students to pursue independent learning. This online diary gives them the opportunity to post entries that can be read by anyone in the school community. It is the means by which students can produce evidence for the different elements of Clio's Challenge—writing a review of a historical novel or a film, visiting a museum with family and friends, attending a Civil War re-enactment, and so on.

The **lesson** in Moodle might at first just appear to be a series of linked web pages. For the History teacher however, it is a wonderful opportunity to blend resources, including images, podcasts, and videos, with questions. Used creatively, the lesson captures a teacher's unique expertise and passion for a subject and preserves it electronically. Moodle lessons give the teacher the opportunity to create rich content that students will want to return to more than once in order to refresh their understanding or sharpen their focus on a particular topic. The lesson can be used to introduce topics, support independent learning, or act as an ideal revision tool.

Approaching the lesson

We plan to introduce our Year 7 History class to the idea of the Doomsday Book as a means by which William reinforced his control over the country. William was naturally curious about the country he had just conquered. He was particularly keen to find out how much it was worth. He despatched officials to every village with detailed questions to ask about the land that they worked on and the animals that they farmed with. He also sent soldiers who threatened to kill people who lied. All of the records from these village surveys were collated into the Doomsday Book. Many Saxons detested the process and the name of the book is derived from this attitude of loathing towards something they regarded as intrusive and unfair. William died before the process could be completed.

Clear lesson objectives can be stated at the start of the lesson.

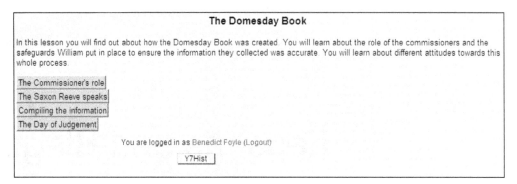

Students would be expected to work through each page and answer questions identical to those found in the Quiz module.

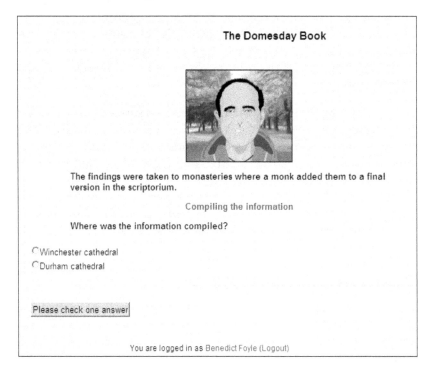

The lesson gives students the opportunity to return to a page if the required level of understanding has not been achieved. The lesson questions help students to reach an understanding at their own pace.

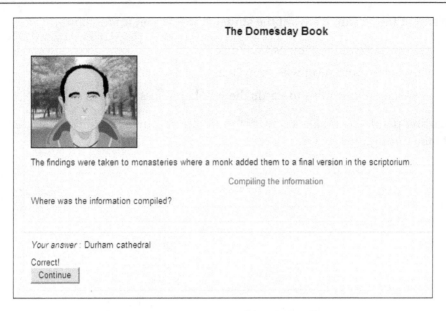

The short video clips we intend to use will come from the excellent National Archive website. It has links to short sequences of approximately ninety seconds in which actors take on the role of villagers and commissioners and offer a variety of opinions about the nature and purpose of the survey that they are taking part in.

At the end of the lesson, we want the students to have an understanding of:

- The purpose of the Domesday Book
- How the information was compiled
- A variety of attitudes towards the whole process

Our starting point is to create a flow diagram that captures the routes a student might take through the lesson:

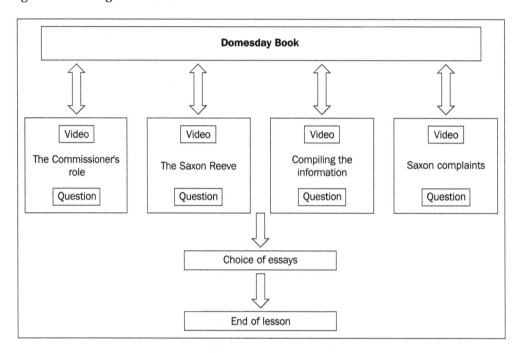

The students will see the set of objectives, a short introduction to the Doomsday Book, and a table of contents. They can select the videos in any order. When they have watched each video and answered the questions associated with the content they will be asked to write longer answers to a series of summative questions. These answers are marked individually by the teacher who thus gets a good overall idea of how well the students have absorbed the information. The assessment of these questions could easily include our essay outcomes marking scale used in our chapter about the Gradebook. The lesson ends when the student has completed all of the answers. The lesson requires:

- A branch table (the table of contents).
- Four question pages based upon a common template.
- One end of branch page.
- A question page for the longer answers.
- An end of lesson page.

The lesson awards marks for the correct answers to questions on each page in much the same way as if they were part of a quiz. Since we are only adding one question per page the scores for these questions are of less significance than a student's answers to the essay questions at the end of the lesson. It is after all, these summative questions that allow the students to demonstrate their understanding of the content they have been working with. Moodle allows this work to be marked in exactly the same way as if it was an essay. This time it will be in the form of an online essay and will take up its place in the Gradebook. We are, therefore, not interested in a standard mark for the students' participation in the lesson and when we set the lesson up, this will become apparent through the choices we make.

Setting up a lesson

It is important to have a clear idea of the lesson structure before starting the creation of the lesson. We have used paper and pen to create a flow diagram. We know which images, videos, and text are needed on each page and have a clear idea of the formative and summative questions that will enable us to challenge our students and assess how well they have understood the significance of the Doomsday Book. We are now in a position to create the lesson:

1. Enter the Year 7 History course and turn on editing.
2. In **Topic 1**, select **Add an Activity** and click **Lesson**.
3. In the **Name** section, enter an unambiguous name for the lesson as this is the text that students will click on to enter the lesson.

4. Enter the values as shown in the following screenshot:

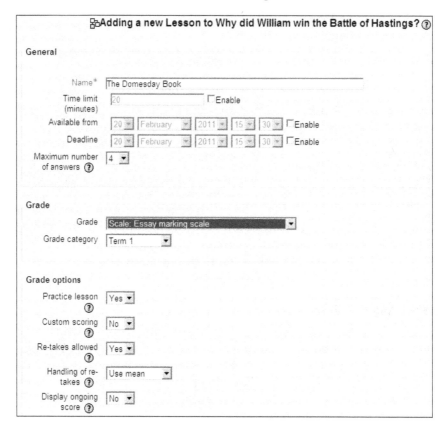

°   In the **General** section, we do not want to impose a time limit on the lesson. We do need to state how many options there are likely to be on each question page. For multiple choice questions, there are usually four options.

°   In the **Grade** section, we want the essay that they compose at the end of the lesson to be marked in the same way that other essays have been marked.

°   In the **Grade options**, our preference is to avoid using the lesson questions as an assessment activity. We want it to be a practice lesson where students can work through the activities without needing to earn a score. We have turned off scoring. The students' final essay submission will be marked in line with our marking policy. Students can retake it as many times as they want to.

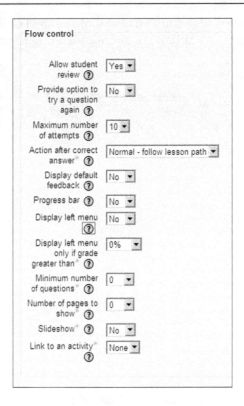

○ In the **Flow control** section, we have clicked the **Show advanced**
   button to see all of the options available. We want students to
   be able to navigate the pages to check answers and go back to
   review answers if necessary. They can take the lesson as often as
   they want as we intend it to be used for revision purposes for a
   timed essay or in the summer examination. We have ignored the
   opportunity to add features such as menus and progress bars as
   we will be creating our own navigation system.

This section also concerns the look and feel of the pages if set to a slide show, an option we are not planning to use.

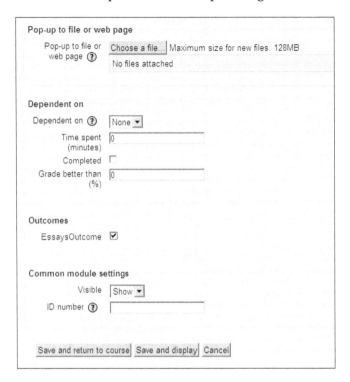

- ° We are planning to create a web link on each page rather than have students download files so we will not be using the **Pop-up to file or web page** option. If you are concerned about the stability of your Internet connection for the weblinks to videos you plan to show, there is an alternative option. This would involve downloading the files to your computer and converting them to .flv files. They can then be uploaded to the file picker in the usual way and a link can be created to each one using the **Choose a file** button shown here. Moodle's video player would play the videos and you would not be reliant on an unstable Internet connection to see the results.

- ○ The **Dependent on** section allows further restrictions to be imposed that are not appropriate for this lesson. We do however, want to mark the essay that will be submitted in accordance with the custom marking scheme developed earlier in the course. The box in the **Outcomes** section must be checked.

- ○ Clicking the **Save and return to course** button ensures that the newly created lesson, **The Domesday Book**, awaits in **Topic 1**.

Creating content

Clicking on the link that has appeared in Topic 1 enables you to create a question page.

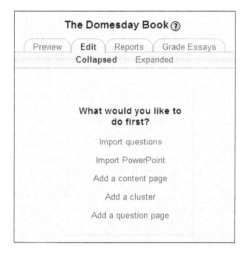

The key to the next section, adding content, is to do things in the correct order to ensure navigation works and does not require a great deal of editing and retesting. In this respect, we plan to:

- Create the four question pages with their content and their questions
- Create the content page which holds a table of contents
- Link the buttons on the contents page to the correct pages
- Add the end of branch page
- Ensure that the essay question links to the end of the lesson

Creating a Question page

Question pages require some content and a quiz question such as true/false, multiple choice, matching, short answer, essay, and so on. Again, it is an important and time saving option to know what you plan to put on each question page.

The question pages with video links will have the same format as in the following image.

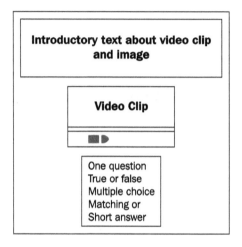

We shall start with the Commissioner's page and ask a multiple choice question regarding the best description for the Commissioner's role in the survey.

1. Click the link in Topic 1 '**The Domesday Book**'.
2. Click the **Add a Question Page** option.
3. Select the **Multiple Choice** option from the drop-down menu.
4. Click the **Add a question page** button.

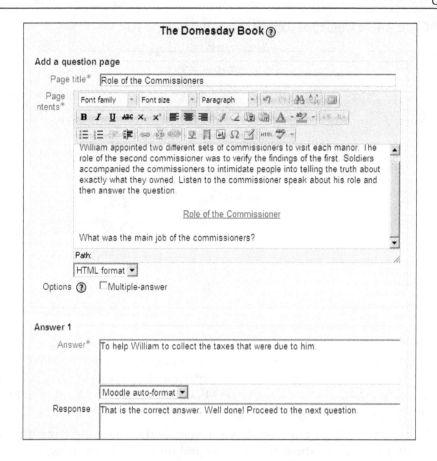

We have given the page a title that will later become a clickable link. We have introduced the commissioner's role briefly. If we wanted to introduce an image here, we would use the method outlined in the second chapter using the **Insert image** button in the HTML editor. In the center of the page, we have inserted a web link to the actual web page where the video can be found. Underneath the link to the video, we have entered the multiple choice question. Several boxes have appeared below the question and they need to be completed in much the same way as we would complete any multiple choice question in the quiz module. Provide alternative answers and make sure with the correct answer that you click on the **next page** option.

5. Click **Add a question page** at the bottom of the page.

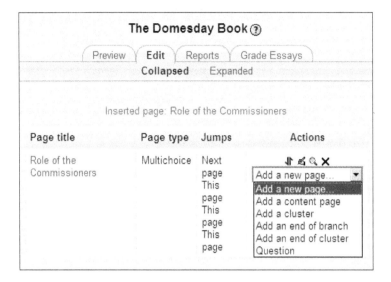

Exercise

1. Repeat steps 2–5 of the Create a Question page section for the three remaining videos, remembering to experiment with different question types for each question page. Use the HTML editor's **Insert image** button to insert an image into the page.

2. The expanded Edit window should resemble the following screenshot where we have used a mixture of true/false and multiple choice questions.

The Domesday Book ⑦

| Preview | **Edit** | Reports | Grade Essays |

Collapsed   Expanded

Inserted page: Day of Judgement

Page title	Page type	Jumps	Actions
Role of the Commissioners	Multichoice	Next page This page This page This page	⬍ ✎ 🔍 ✗ Add a new page... ▾
The Saxon Reeve	True/false	Next page This page	⬍ ✎ 🔍 ✗ Add a new page... ▾
Compiling the information	Multichoice	Next page This page	⬍ ✎ 🔍 ✗ Add a new page... ▾
Day of Judgement	True/false	Next page This page	⬍ ✎ 🔍 ✗ Add a new page... ▾

Inserting a web link

Why are we using a web link on each question page? A web link takes the student straight to the relevant website where the videos are hosted. Assuming the Internet connection is good, students can click on the video clip format that suits their machine. It is sometimes, though not always, possible to embed a video clip if the website provides the necessary code. YouTube offers this facility although it is not available with our videos from the National Archives site. Conveniently, however, there is a transcript available from the site if the student cannot play the video clip for any reason.

Equally, if you have video clips that you wish to use yourself, they can be uploaded to the course using the same method explained earlier and the video can be played from the files area of the Moodle site. Thus, instead of a web link on the question page, there will be a hyperlink to a file which opens automatically in a separate window. It is a matter of experimenting and finding out which method works best for you and your students. Video is a vital element in the delivery of lessons. Consider the following examples of Moodle lessons where video and podcast resources are pivotal to the success of the lesson:

- Why did people fight in the Civil War? The video clips consist of interviews recorded with participants at a Civil War re-enactment event.

- What were the aims of the Big Three going into the Treaty of Versailles? Short podcasts outline the different aims and objectives of Wilson, Lloyd George, and Clemenceau as they prepared to formulate the peace treaty in 1919.

- Why did people vote for Hitler? A mixture of short video clips and podcasts present the reasoning of different individuals such as an unemployed teenager, an army veteran, and the owner of a small business.

Follow these instructions for creating web links to the videos available on the National Archive website.

1. Highlight the text that will become the web link.

   ° For page two, this could be 'The Saxon Reeve speaks' and for page four it could be 'The Day of Judgement'.

2. Click the **Insert Web Link** option on the toolbar (it is to the left of the symbol of a broken chain).

3. In the dialog box, enter the URL of the web page. It can be copied and pasted directly from the address bar of the browser.

4. Enter an appropriate title for the link.

5. Set **Target** to **New Window**.

6. Click **Insert**.

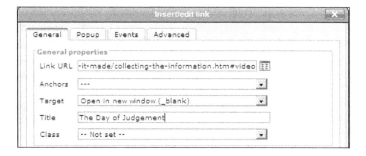

Adding a contents page

Having created the four question pages, we need to create a contents page which will act like a table of contents for the lesson. This would also be a suitable location for lesson objectives in the form of a bulleted list. This will provide an important link between the opening of the lesson and the crucial activity at the end of the lesson where students answer the summative question and are able to demonstrate their understanding of the significance of the Doomsday Book.

1. Click the **Edit** tab.

2. Click the **Expanded** option.

3. Click **Add a content page**.

4. Enter **The Doomsday Book** in the **Page title** section.

5. Write a brief introduction to the lesson in the **Page contents** section.

6. In **Content 1**, enter **The Commissioner's role** — this will be the text that will appear on the button.

7. In **Jump,** select **Role of the Commissioners** from the drop-down menu — when the button is clicked, the correct page will open.

8. Repeat steps 6-7 for the three remaining pages, remembering to start in **Content 2**.

9. Click the **Add a question page** button.

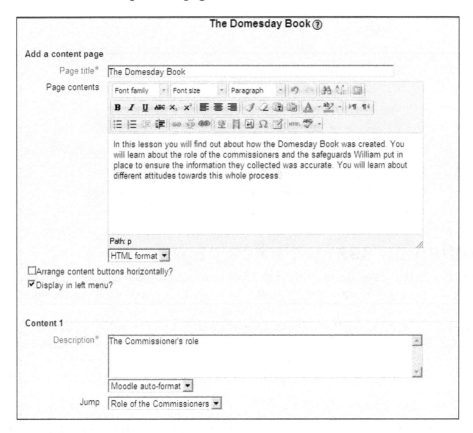

The contents page will now appear in its correct place in front of the four question pages in the expanded **Edit** window.

Adding an essay choice page

The students will have learned about the role of the commissioners and the reeve during the process and also about various attitudes to the process. They also need to submit a piece of writing to show their understanding of the content they have studied. This piece of work will be submitted directly to us for marking and grading in the Gradebook according to the marking scale we created in the **Outcomes** section. This is a neat and tidy way of assessing how well the students have understood the content. Submitting this piece of work will effectively end the lesson for each student.

1. Open the lesson **Edit** tab.

2. Navigate to the bottom of the screen where the page for the final question page can be found.

3. Click **Add a question page.**

4. Select **Essay** as the question type.

5. Give it the name **Choice of essay questions.**

6. Enter appropriate essay questions in the **Page contents** section.

7. Link this question to an **End of lesson page**.

8. Click the **Add a question page** button.

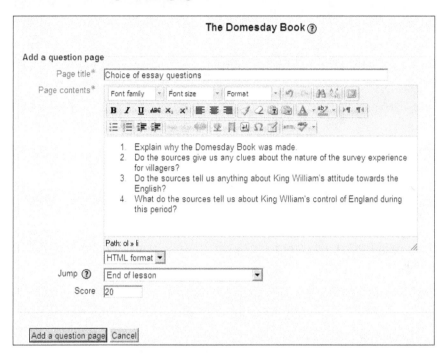

Adding an end of branch page

In the **Edit** tab, it is necessary to add an **end of branch page** after the final video question page and before the essay questions. From the **end of branch page**, it will be possible to link to the final question page involving the selection of essay questions about the videos the students will have watched. This page is already linked to an end of lesson page.

1. Open the lesson **Edit** page.

2. Navigate to the bottom of the screen where the page for the final video question page can be found.

3. Click on **Add an end of branch**.

4. In **Page title** enter **The essay section.**

5. In the **Page contents** section, explain that the lesson will now move to a selection of essay questions based on the videos.

6. Link this page to the essay questions page.

7. Click **Save page**.

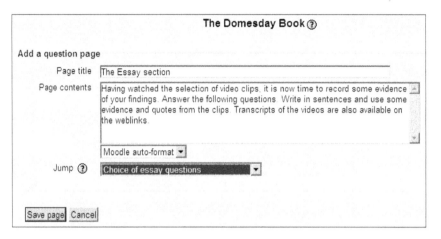

When students have worked through and answered the four sections the **end of branch** page will inform them of their next task and direct them to the selection of essay questions.

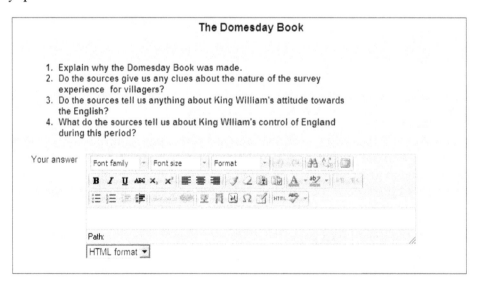

The questions can be completed onscreen and submitted. The teacher will be able to mark the answers and give feedback by going into the Gradebook and using the same techniques to assess work as described in Chapter 6.

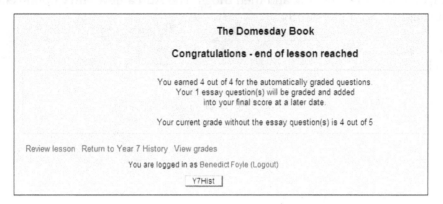

Patience is required with the preparation of lessons and it is necessary to test them out thoroughly before unleashing them on your students. Use of the **Preview** tab is essential in this regard. The E**dit** tab allows you to make the necessary changes.

Lessons come to life when a teacher's expertise is captured in the question page contents and a structure is built that challenges the students to take different routes. The number of question pages and branches is limitless but care must be taken to work within the lesson objectives in order to achieve success. Careful selection of formative and summative questions is essential if a Moodle lesson is to be a valuable learning experience. Dead ends can only be avoided by careful planning and testing!

Blogs

The phenomenon that is blogging has had an impact on education in a variety of ways, mainly through its creative use by teachers to give an audience to their own and students' work. It is very easy for a student to create and maintain a blog within Moodle. Blog entries about books read, visits undertaken, and podcasts created with a historical theme are striking evidence of a capacity for independent learning.

Creating a blog entry

Once a student has an account on the school's Moodle, their blog is available by clicking on the **My Profile** link and then **Blogs.** The **Add a new entry** option enables them to begin blogging instantly.

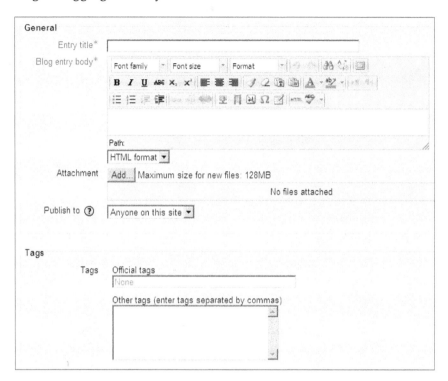

The student can include attachments such as video clips or podcasts made about a particular visit. They can insert images directly into the blog but must be reminded to resize images so that they are not too large. If people are going to read the blog they do not want to scroll across huge images. It is also possible to link the blog entry to a collection of Flickr images or a Facebook page. The images should follow similar rules mentioned in earlier chapters. The other important choice concerns publishing options. Students have the choice to publish only to themselves or to everyone on the site. They might use the former if the entry is still being drafted or indeed if they do not want anyone else to read it.

Creating blog entries for the Year 7 History course only

We may want to set up the opportunity for our students to post a blog entry specifically to the Year 7 History course. Students may have visited a location, museum, or venue of relevance to the course, read a book, watched a TV program with a connection to the medieval period, or found out a useful fact in conversation. Posting a blog entry would be an appropriate way of recording this experience. At present, a teacher and student can post an entry to their blog and they both have the option to publish it to the whole site or simply to themselves. We are creating a separate blog for Year 7 History students to share with each other rather than the whole site.

In order to make this possible on the Year 7 History course, the administrator needs to make some changes to the settings in the **Site administration** link. Primarily, the administrator needs to ensure that the Blog menu is available for teachers to apply to the course. This can be achieved by following the sequence below:

1. Click **Site administration**.
2. Click **plugins**.
3. Click **blocks**.
4. Click **manage blocks**.
5. Ensure that the eye symbols beside **Blog menu, Blog tags** and **Comments** are open.

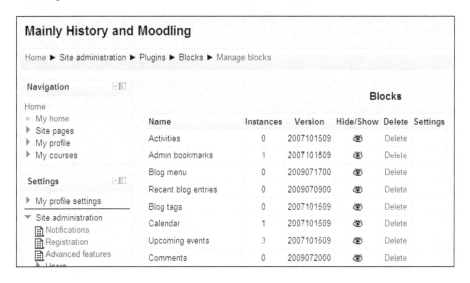

- ° It is possible for students to add comments to blogs and equally the **Comments** block can be used to add comments to virtually any activity in Moodle.

Adding a Blog menu block to the course

The teacher is now in a position to add a Blog menu block to the course so that students can post entries to this specific course. It is important to stress that this blog entry will still be visible throughout the site.

1. Enter the Year 7 History course and turn on editing.
2. In the **Add a block** dropdown select **Blog menu.**
3. Click the **Configuration** icon.
4. Use the familiar options to determine the position of the block in the left- or right-hand pane.
5. Click **Save changes**.

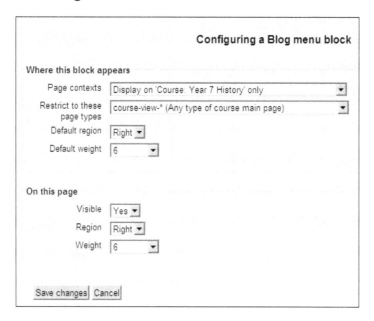

When a student logs in to the course the Blog menu is available. The options are straightforward.

- The first option lists all blog entries within the course.

- The second option lists only the student's own entries in the course.

- The third option allows a student to add an entry to the Year 7 History course.

- The fourth option allows the student to view every blog entry that he or she has made.

- BFoyle wishes to add an entry to the course about a visit to Clifford's Tower in York. He clicks **Add an entry about this course** and completes the post in the normal way. At the end of the post there will be a tick box which must be checked to associate the entry with the Year 7 History course.

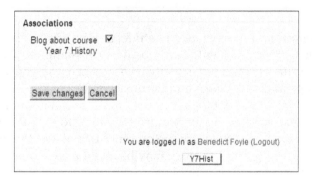

When another student JFoyle logs in to the course and clicks on the link to **View all entries for this course,** she will see BFoyle's entry and has the option to use the comment box if she desires. Teachers can easily delete comments where necessary.

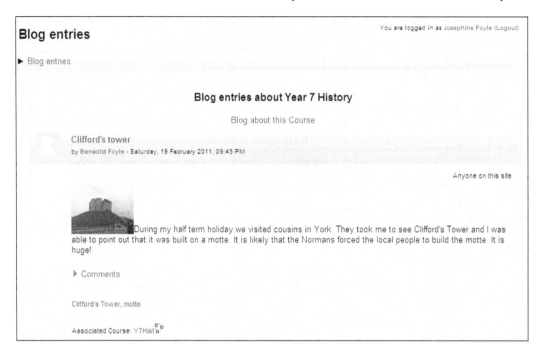

A blog is a marvellous tool in the hands of students who want to set down their ideas in diary form. The fact that each entry is date and time stamped makes it a valuable tool. Nowadays, students could realistically be asked at a university interview to demonstrate a longstanding interest and enthusiasm for History. Students should be encouraged to think of every blog entry they make as having potentially huge significance. Each one could be the very entry they refer to in that crucial interview question which demonstrates their unique qualities or unlocks the door to the position they are applying for. The entry may be about a television or radio program, a visit, or a book that inspired or provoked a reaction. Whatever the content, the entry should be carefully constructed and concern a topic or issue that is of genuine interest to them.

The blog tool is a powerful means by which students can reflect on their learning or share knowledge and understanding. They are writing for a specific audience which always helps to give purpose and direction to their entries. It is a classic tool that is tailor made for gifted and talented students to shine as they have the option of creating a journal for themselves alone or for a much wider audience and can adapt their writing style accordingly.

Another exciting feature of the blog tool is that Moodle allows teachers to create links to external blogs. This option is available in the **My profile** settings under **Blogs** and **External blogs.** It is useful if a teacher wants to draw attention to the work of another colleague who blogs regularly on similar areas of interest. It works in an identical way to the **RSS feeds** that we created in an earlier chapter.

Summary

In this chapter, we have looked at the lesson module and the blog module. Both provide different learning experiences for students, encourage independent learning, and can be used to test a host of different skills for students and teachers alike! For teachers, the reusability of carefully constructed lessons is very appealing. For students, a blog that is maintained properly has the potential to yield invaluable evidence in years to come.

In the next chapter, we shall look at a tool that has been mentioned in this chapter briefly as a valuable addition to lessons, the podcast. I use the open source audio editing package called Audacity to create podcasts for my lessons. The creation of Moodle courses tends to drive teachers to look at alternative ways of presenting content to students and the results are often innovative and daring. For example, the website www.prezi.com allows teachers and students to create dynamic presentations that are worlds away from the slide-based formula behind most presentations shown on whiteboards. Prezis are easy to create and embed into Moodle courses. Similarly, at www.glogster.com it is possible to create interactive posters that can light up a course for students instantly. Again, they are straightforward to create and easy to embed within Moodle courses. We shall look at another open source package which in its way is an alternative to the lesson module in Moodle. It is called Xerte and is an attractive option because of the content-rich nature of the learning objects that can be created and then used within a Moodle course.

8

Using Xerte and Audacity

Xerte enables rich interactive learning resources to be created quickly and seamlessly. Producing a resource involves creating a series of interlinked pages. Navigation is far more straightforward for those of you who were mystified by the lesson's branch tables and question pages.

The pages are packaged in a folder and can be uploaded as a ZIP file and a link to the **index.htm** file ensures that the learning resource will roll out. We have practised such skills in earlier chapters.

Why do I like Xerte? The materials produced have a professional finish that the developers of some commercial software would do well to replicate. There are also a series of accessibility options which make it useful for a whole range of students with different learning styles and needs. The slides created can be viewed in a variety of color formats, font sizes, and font types at the click of a button. Xerte integrates multimedia seamlessly and enables work to be done on images that can bring lessons to life. Xerte does enable any activity to provide feedback on what was achieved successfully and what was less effective. It is an application built by a team of enthusiastic educators intent upon capturing a teacher's expertise using electronic resources. The feedback options alone capture that expertise and make a learning resource truly reusable. The rich interactive learning experiences can be quickly and easily generated at the hands of a willing and dedicated teacher.

Xerte

Created by a team at Nottingham University, Xerte is a piece of open source software that can be used as an alternative to creating lessons in Moodle. The software is freely available to download at the Nottingham University website.

Xerte takes the Moodle lesson a stage further, providing a dynamic multimedia learning experience. Time invested early on produces rich pages with a wide variety of templates including drag-and-drop quizzes and image hot spots.

If the Moodle lesson whetted your appetite then take the bait and download Xerte onto your machine. It will be a rewarding journey. A once hidden gem is now an important tool being employed effectively by more and more educators.

Downloading Xerte

Full installation of Xerte Online Toolkits on a server requires administrator's permissions. That may require some negotiation so a logical first step would be to install the latest Xerte download from the Nottingham University website onto a standalone machine. After creating some learning resources and getting a feel for the software, then might be the time to approach your administrator in order to roll out the full network version.

Installation is straightforward if you go with the default settings.

Making a plan

It is important to have a clear idea of the interactive content you wish to build in order to make the implementation process swift and straightforward. Prepare image files and resize them so that they are anything between 100 and 200 KB. We saw how to do this in Chapter 2. Audio files can be broken down into chunks so that they do not take too long to download. We shall see how to do this using **Audacity** later in the chapter. Name each file carefully if you're planning to use them in a Xerte learning object. Later, we shall see how to link a page to images in **Flickr** and this requires effective use of its tagging facility.

Each learning resource in Xerte becomes a project and when it is ready to be published on your Moodle course, it will resemble a book made up of several pages of content. In this section, we are going to put together some resources for our Year 7 class to learn about the origins and purpose of medieval castles, prior to a school trip to Caerphilly Castle. We shall include a table of contents so students can find different sections easily, pages with images and explanations, and opportunities to use drag-and-drop techniques to match terms and their descriptions. This approach will also signpost other useful page templates available. We shall concentrate upon using images and see how straightforward it is to create a variety of tasks and activities with them. The resource that we build would be useful for students who are unavailable for the trip as well as students who take part in it and students who simply want a revision tool.

We shall create:

- A page showing the contents and a title
- An image of a castle and some text
- An image of a portcullis with an audio soundtrack, text, and a magnifier
- A drag-and-drop matching activity
- An interactive diagram
- A link to Flickr images of Caerphilly Castle
- A page using three columns for use when making comparisons
- A multiple choice quiz

The pages can be created quickly, uploaded to the Moodle course easily, and reused by students as often as they need.

Creating the opening page

When double-clicking the Xerte icon on our desktop, we get the following screen:

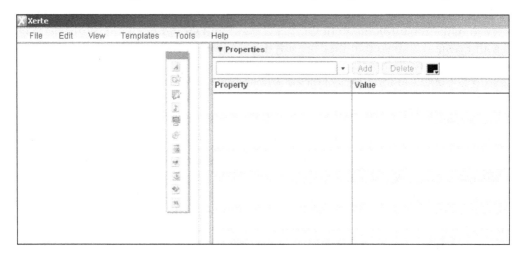

Selecting the **Templates** | **Page Templates** option forces us to create a folder where the project and all the resources it will use are to be stored. In the example below, we have chosen to save our work in a folder called MedievalCastles on the desktop.

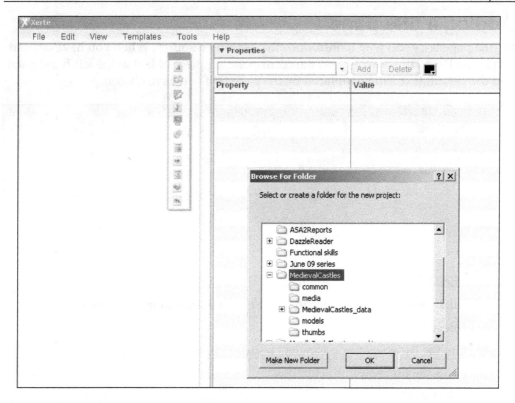

The learning object needs an initial page to define how the resource is going to be used. Take a look at the following screen to see the choices that are available.

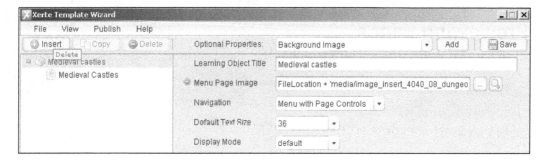

We have given the learning object a title — Medieval Castles.

To insert a background image, we have selected that option from the **Optional Properties**. Clicking **Add** allows us to select the image. The menu page image allows you to select the image to use. It is important to resize images so that they do not obscure the links that will be generated on the **Main Menu** page. Remember as a rule of thumb to keep image size to between 100 and 200 KB.

Adding a title page

A Title page is a good way to introduce the learning resource. When you have entered text in the Page Title box, click on the corresponding piece of text in the left-hand pane and the default text will be replaced by the page title you have chosen.

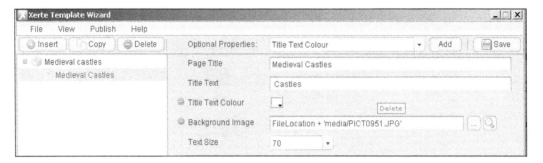

1. Click **Insert | Text | Title page**.
2. Click **Optional Properties** to select the background image option.
3. Select **Add**.
4. Use the **Browse** option to select a suitable image.
5. Enter the title text in the textbox.
6. Select **Add**.
7. Click **Optional Properties** to select the **Title** text color.
8. Click **Save**.

Previewing pages

Click the **Play** option in the bottom of the right-hand corner.

Notice the accessibility options along the bottom of the slide. The page controls in the top right-hand corner will appear on each page. The **Medieval Castles** link is the first one to appear and as pages are added a link will be generated on the **Main Menu** page for each page that is created.

Clicking the **Medieval Castles** link takes us to:

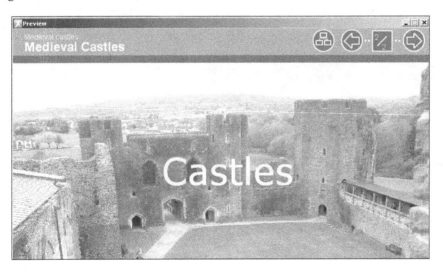

The white text appears as expected. An image of this size may take time to download. The learning object now has some content and we can start adding more pages using the **Insert** option. The range of templates that a teacher can use is extensive. It is beyond the remit of this book to show how they can all be used but it is certainly possible to show a range to get you interested in the possibilities.

Creating a page with an image, sound, and magnifer

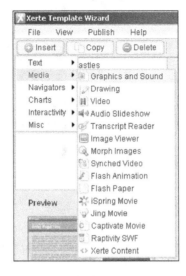

We want to create a page with an image and text but also the option for a student to listen to the text. In order to do this we need to have the text, audio file and image ready to insert into the page. We select the required template from **Insert | Media | Graphics and sound** option.

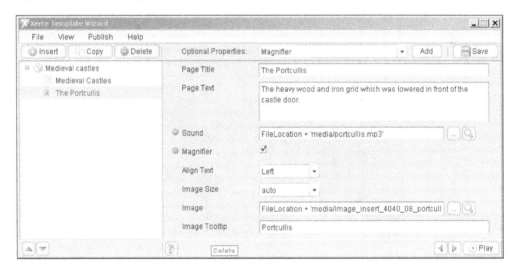

We have added a limited amount of text to the page. We have inserted the image and added a tool tip. The sound and magnifier options were obtained using the **Optional Properties** dropdown and the **Add** button. The sound option will allow sound controls to be included on the page. The difference between the **Sound** and **Narration** option is that the former gives the user a choice and the latter plays as soon as the page has loaded. The **Magnifier** will allow students to take a closer look at the image of the portcullis. The finished page therefore gives students many accessibility options along the base of the page. These include the choice of reading or having the content read and the chance to scrutinize the image more closely if they choose. A link to the portcullis page will automatically have been inserted in the **Main Menu** page.

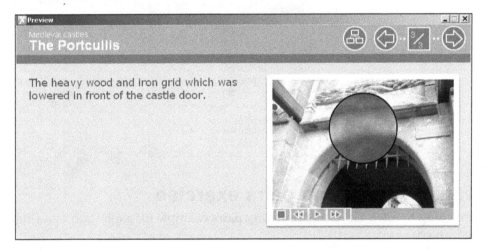

The opportunity to listen to the text that they can see before them is reassuring for those students who struggle to read independently. For many, it brings the topic to life and enables them to put down their ideas in more detail and with greater confidence when it comes to written work. In the next section, we shall look in detail at how to create the sound files using Audacity. We shall also see that it is not a time consuming process and one that is greatly appreciated by many students. Xerte gives the option to highlight text as it is narrated and the option to create hotspots on images so extra information can be included on the page. It is simply a case of finding the template that does what you want and setting the preferences for it.

Xerte provides a very useful **Preview** of each page template when you hover the mouse on any entry in the drop-down menu. On the **Media** menu alone there are options, among others, to include pages with video (flv files are recommended).

Pages with interactivity

There are a variety of options for interactive pages:

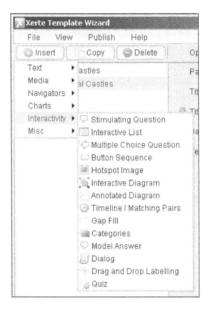

Creating a matching pairs exercise

We are going to use a **Timeline/Matching pairs** example for a question covering castle features.

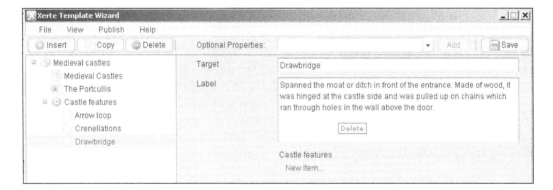

We want students to be able to drag the correct description to the correct place on the page. By clicking **New item** we can add as many target words and descriptions as we need.

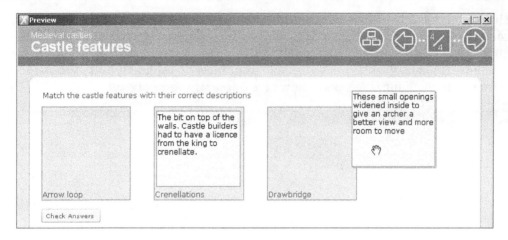

The finished exercise allows students to check their own answers. Feedback comments can also be included.

Inserting an annotated diagram

An annotated diagram allows the user to click on a choice of links beside an image. Immediately, the relevant textbox pops up with an arrow linking it to the related part of the diagram.

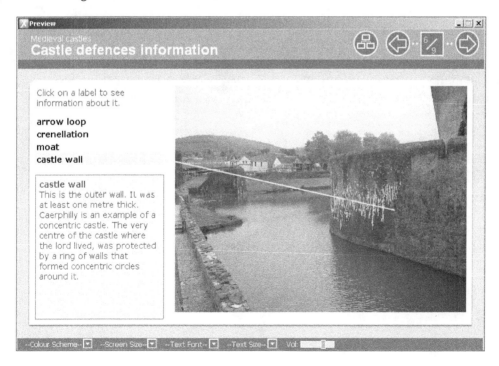

History teachers recognize the opportunities this template offers to recreate the vital components of worksheets that have worked successfully for years and could now quite easily be transformed into equally valuable interactive experiences for the same students. The image template is available from **Insert | Interactivity | Annotated image**. The following screenshot shows the important components.

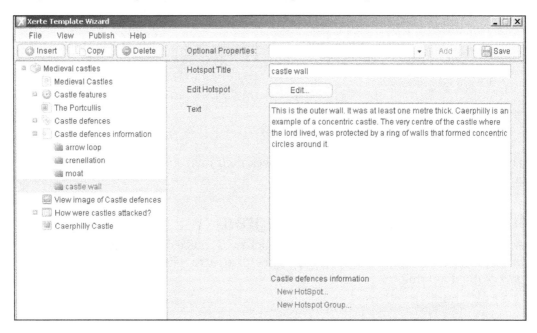

Each hotspot on the image requires its own title and descriptive text. The hotspot is placed in the correct position on the page when you click on **Edit Hotspot** and move or resize the yellow box that appears. Clicking **Save** adds the hotspot to the page and it appears in the left-hand pane. The next hotspot is created by clicking the **New Hotspot** link.

Creating a drag-and-drop labelling exercise

Another exercise for which History teachers can easily spot potential is the drag-and-drop labeling activity as featured in the following screenshot. It shows the same image and labels rather than links that can be clicked on to reveal text. This time when the student places the label in the correct position, the text about the label is revealed.

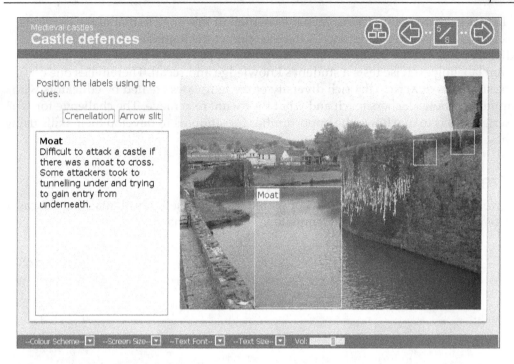

The yellow boxes appear in preview mode but do not appear when students are attempting the actual exercise. This template is obtained by clicking **Insert | Interactivity | Drag and drop labelling**.

The following screenshot shows the page being set up:

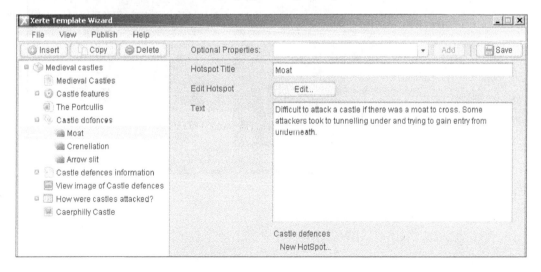

There is no significant difference in the creation of this page to that of the previous example. The one key difference is the selection of the template. The annotated diagram lays out the information with clarity and purpose while the drag-and-drop labeling exercise tests a student's knowledge and recall. Therein lies one of the strengths of Xerte—the rich diversity of the templates created by educators who appreciate how teachers teach and what they want to achieve. The challenge for Xerte users is to maximize the opportunities for students to develop their skills using these fantastic pedagogical tools.

Creating a three-column page

If we wanted to create a page that compared different methods of attacking the castle defences, then there is an ideal template for doing just that.

It is available by clicking **Insert | Navigators | Column page**. You will notice the similarities with previous pages in the setup page.

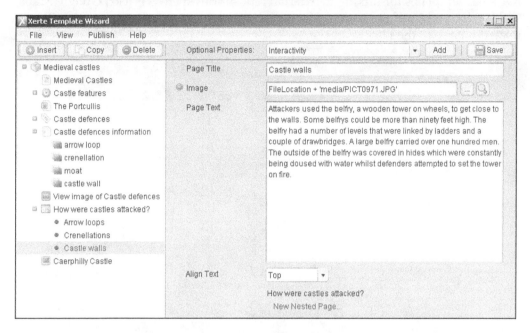

Each column requires its own page and is reached by clicking the **New nested page** link. Each column also requires an image and that is obtained by clicking the **Optional Properties** dropdown and selecting **Image** and **Add.** It is then possible to browse for the required image.

It is possible to create tabbed pages rather than columns if space is an issue. This can be done by selecting the required template from **Insert | Navigator | Tabbed navigator.** Other navigable options include using buttons or a slideshow or an accordion navigator that consists of vertical rather than horizontal tabs.

Linking to external repositories

Xerte has templates for linking to external repositories such as **Flickr**, **Google Maps**, **Wikipedia**, and **Youtube Video**. The following screenshot shows a page that links to related images in the Flickr website.

If we use tags for the required images, it prevents most anomalies from occurring. The setup page works if the required tags are entered in the **Keywords** section.

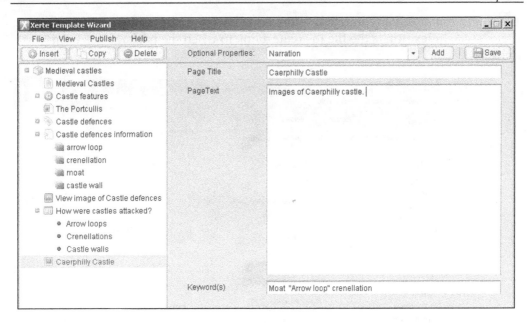

Publishing Medieval Castles on Moodle

The Xerte Learning Object, Medieval Castles, can be published when we are satisfied with our pages. In the **Publish** menu, there are two options: **Publish** and **Package**. The latter option deals with uploading **Scorm** compliant packages that we shall look at later in the chapter. Clicking on **Publish** brings up the following screen:

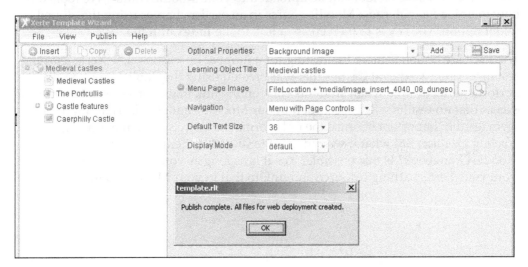

The folder contains many files and folders that have built up as the project has progressed. **Index.htm** is the file to create a link to when the package has been uploaded.

The Medieval Castles folder can be uploaded to your Moodle course. We looked at how to upload a folder to a Moodle course in an earlier chapter using the zipped folder option. The key is to then create a link to the **index.htm** file.

The **Package** option is more interesting for a number of reasons. The Xerte learning resource called Medieval Castles that was created using the Publish option will perform perfectly well when students click on the link that opens the `index.htm` file except that no results will be recorded in our Moodle Gradebook. That might not seem terribly important because the only formative exercise was the drag-and-drop labeling exercise. But what if we did want to record student performance in our Moodle Gradebook? Is this possible? Yes it is as long as you create a Scorm package from your Xerte learning resource and link to that in your Moodle course.

Creating a Scorm package

A Scorm package is one which is built to a technical standard for e-learning and is thus capable of operating within any **Learning Management System**. **Hot Potatoes** software is capable of generating quizzes as Scorm packages. Xerte learning resources need to include a quiz or multiple choice page in order to create a Scorm package. The results from the quiz or multiple choice exercise will appear in the Moodle Gradebook when a student has completed an activity.

Creating a quiz page

We are going to create a quiz page called 'Castles quiz' containing several questions including the following example:

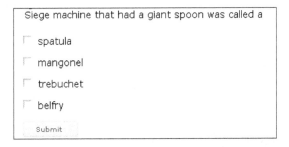

We will start by inserting a quiz page.

1. Click **Insert**.
2. Click **Interactivity**.
3. Click **Quiz**.
4. Click **Optional properties**.
5. Select **Scorm tracking** from the dropdown.
6. Click **Add**.
7. In the **Scorm tracking** dropdown, select **Track last score**.

8. Complete the remaining elements as in the following screenshot:

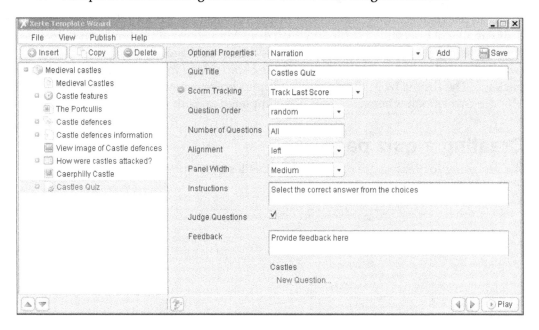

9. Click **New Question** to enter details of the first question as in the following screenshot:

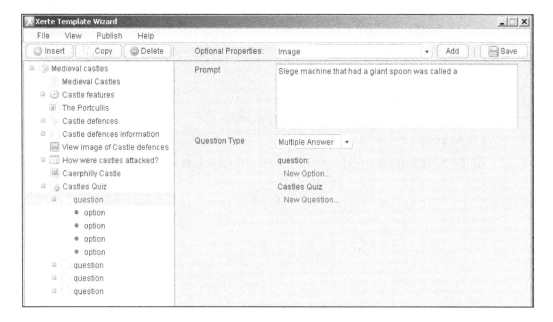

10. Click **New option** to enter the first possible answer as in the following screenshot:

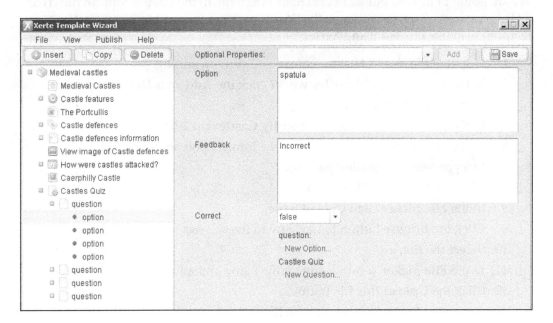

11. Repeat step 10 to add the correct answer 'Mangonel'.

12. Repeat step 10 again to add the incorrect answer 'trebuchet'.

13. Repeat step 10 again to add the incorrect answer 'belfry'.

14. Click **Save**.

15. Add three further questions by repeating steps 9 to 14 for each multiple choice question.

Creating the ZIP file for the Scorm package

To create the Scorm package so that it is ready for uploading to our Year 7 History course, we need to build a ZIP file and save it for example, on our desktop ready for the next phase.

1. Click **Publish**.

2. Click **Package**.

3. Save the ZIP file with a suitable filename in a suitable location.

Uploading the scorm package

We are going to upload our `WalesTrip2011.zip` file to the Castles topic in our Year 7 History course. This file contains the Scorm package for our Medieval Castles learning resource created using Xerte.

1. Log in to the Year 7 History course and turn on editing.
2. In the Topic **How did castles work?** click the **Add an activity** dropdown.
3. Select **SCORM package**.
4. In the **Name** section enter **Caerphilly Castle trip 2011**.
5. In the **Description** section enter some information about the visit.
6. In **Type** select **Uploaded package**.
7. Click the **Choose a file** button.
8. In the **File picker** click **Upload a file**.
9. Click the **Browse** button to navigate to the `WalesTrip2011.zip` file.
10. **Select the file.**
11. In the **File picker** window enter a file name and add the `.zip` extension.
12. Click the **Upload this file** button.
13. Ignore the **Restrict answering** section.
14. Replicate the settings in the following screenshot:

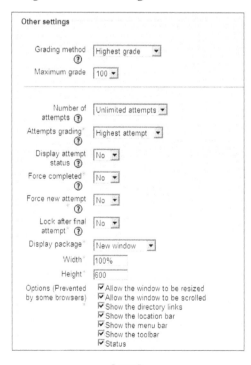

- In **Other settings**, we want to record each student's highest grade regardless of how many times they have attempted the quiz and we want the Gradebook to record the quiz result as a percentage. The remainder of the settings concern the look and behavior of the quiz and we have given the students as much control as they need to make the quiz experience as comfortable as possible.

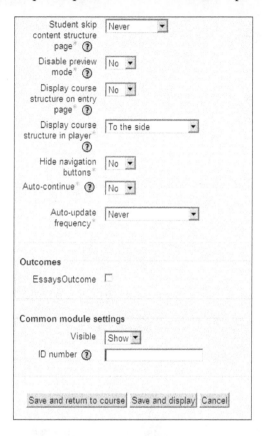

- The remaining settings are worth experimenting with to see the different possible layouts of the quiz. We do not plan to include the quiz in our **Outcomes** marking because it is based solely on multiple choice questions. It is a good idea to give the quiz an **ID number** for use within the Gradebook.

15. Click the **Save and return to course** button.

The Gradebook and the Scorm package

When students log in and perform the quiz, their results are converted into a percentage which they can see as they log out and also in their **Grades** section. In the following screenshot, FFoyle can clearly see that all of her answers were correct.

Equally, when the teacher logs in, the grades of each of the students are clearly visible in the Gradebook.

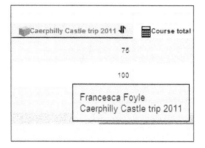

Audacity

Audacity is a tool that students make use of with their eyes closed. Experienced teachers transform the way they teach in seconds once it becomes clear what this piece of software is capable of achieving. It is an audio recording package. At its simplest level, it looks like the interface on your video recorder with its Pause - Play - Stop - Rewind - Forward and Record buttons. Plug in a USB microphone to your PC or laptop and you have a powerful recording tool. Press record, read the text or whatever there is to say and press stop. Save it as an mp3 file and you have something tangible to use in a course. So record that worksheet as an audio file in a couple of minutes. If you make a mistake, find it on the wavy screen, highlight it, and press the *Backspace* to get rid of the noise/dog bark and so on. It is that easy. Keep the files small. Be adventurous and use some of the Audacity tools to introduce fade in and fade out.

Why use Audacity?

Audacity is an open source audio editor. It is free to download and is used to create audio files that form a valuable part of your course. I have used it to record extracts from the radio as well as record the contents of worksheets for use in rich interactive content that is accessible especially to students who read with difficulty. Audacity is the complete audio tool. I use Audacity because it is:

- Open source and free
- Easy to install
- Straightforward to use

Downloading Audacity

I use www.sourceforge.com to locate the option to download. It is a straightforward process:

1. Click the **Download** link.
2. In your **Downloads** folder locate the **setup** file.
3. Double-click it.
4. Accept the default options.
5. Launch Audacity from your desktop.

The Lame Encoder

To save as an mp3 file, you do need to download an extra file and store it in the same folder as your Audacity installation. Instructions for inserting this file, the **Lame Encoder,** are available from the **Help** menu. This file inserts the option to export any file you create to the mp3 format. It adds an important option to the **Export** section on the **File** menu.

It is not tricky and simply requires you to save the file to the folder and then point Audacity to the file on your computer.

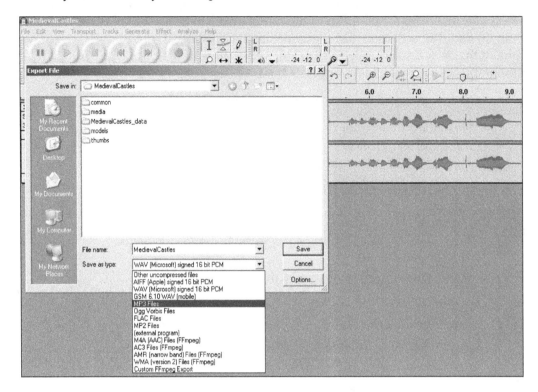

Audacity Essentials

When you open Audacity, you will immediately see the familiar range of six buttons. There are no surprises there.

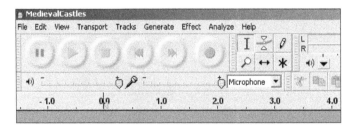

To test whether it works:

1. Plug in a USB microphone.

2. Press the **Record** option.

3. Start talking.

4. Click **Stop** when you have finished.

5. Press **Play** to hear the content.

You have created your first audio file. Various departments in your school may well spend a small fortune on pre-recorded audio files. This is how easy it is to make your own and better versions because you control the whole process from start to finish.

It is important to keep file size under control because you do not want the files to become so large that they take an age to download. Short and sharp is the message.

Simple Audacity Tasks

The following section contains some of the procedures that you will need to get yourself up and running with Audacity. They include simple ways to make your audio file.

Removing unexpected noises in your recording

1. Locate the section in the wavy screen.

2. Select it by dragging the mouse over it.

3. Press the *Backspace* key to remove it.

Using fade in features

1. Select the section that you wish to fade in/out.

2. Go to the **Effects** menu.

3. Select **Fade in.**

4. Save the changes.

5. Play the track to hear the changes.

Using fade out features

Repeat steps 3 – 5 as above selecting the **Fade out** option.

Increasing the volume of the whole track

1. Select the whole track.

2. Go to the **Effects** menu.

3. Select the **Amplify** option.

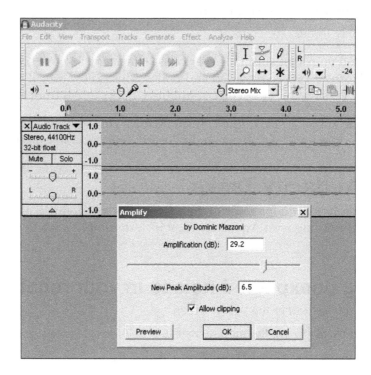

4. Click the slider to increase amplification by a value of 6.5 dB.

5. Check the **Allow clipping** box.

6. Click **OK**.

7. Carefully check to see that the wavy lines have increased in size as in the following screenshot.

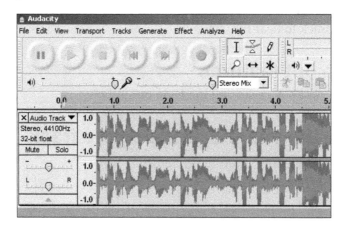

Creating a file from a segment of another track

1. Open the source file.
2. Select the segment.
3. Use the **copy** tool.
4. Open the destination file.
5. Use the **paste** tool.
6. Save the new file.

Inserting a background track

1. Click on **File | Import | Audio**.
2. Navigate to the audio track.
3. Click **Open** and Audacity inserts it into the window in its own track.

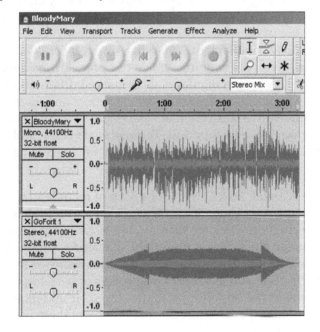

In the example, we have recorded a discussion about a monarch known as Bloody Mary that lasts approximately three minutes. This is represented by the first track. We have imported a soundtrack that lasts a similar length of time and plays at the same time. We know this because it starts and finishes at the same time. The first minute includes a gradual fading in of the soundtrack as shown by the gradually expanding triangular shape at the start. The end of the track shows a contracting triangular shape that represents the gradual fading out of the soundtrack. The discussion continues at the same volume for the three minutes.

Play with Audacity to create small audio tracks that can be used in various modules within Moodle such as lessons, quizzes and forums. They can also be used with learning objects created in Xerte.

Summary

Open source software is available to create high quality interactive resources with ease. Audacity and Xerte are two examples of high quality software that takes away the pain of creating pages of content. Xerte uses an impressive range of templates that have different pedagogical benefits to learners and enable the teacher to find the right balance of resources to fit particular learning strategies. If you want students to be able to read text while listening to a voice recording of the same text in order to reinforce understanding then Xerte provides the templates and Audacity provides the means to easily create the sound file. Together they are a potent means of creating durable learning resources. The reality is that they are free, fun to play with, and a teacher should view them as an artist views the array of tools at his or her disposal to create a masterpiece. The resources that are produced dovetail neatly with Moodle and clearly complement each other. Support for the tools is more prominent now than ever. A host of invaluable resources are available at `http://www.techdis.ac.uk/` including regular webcasts about different uses of Xerte, a forum for teachers who use the software in the classroom and a sandpit area to try out ideas. Xerte is innovative software that clearly has a strong community behind it and is set to develop over a long period. Templates are being added regularly including a recent addition that allows users to enter an extended answer to a question and view a model response.

In the next chapter, we shall look at that all important module in the constructivist teacher's armoury—the workshop. Students are invited to complete a piece of work such as a presentation. They are then invited to carry out a trial assessment of a typical presentation before being randomly allocated assignments to assess within their own peer group. The assessments are then returned to their authors for discussion with their peers and teachers. This process of peer-to-peer assessment gives students an invaluable opportunity to develop their understanding, set themselves realistic and achievable targets, and empower them in crucial decision making about their learning.

Moodle Workshops

In this chapter, we shall look at the role of Moodle workshops and how they can be used to enhance a student's understanding of topics and reinforce good practice. The virtual workshop allows students to assess the work of peers in a controlled and measured way, giving them insight into the breadth and scale of work that can be produced in a particular topic. I like the workshop having seen first hand how it releases time for a teacher to focus on a student's needs while also fostering a mature climate of peer-to-peer assessment. While appearing complex when used for the first time, workshops are definitely worth persevering with. If so, students will reach a stage where they find it normal practice to place their presentation, essay answer, and so on in a workshop knowing that they are going to get valuable and carefully structured feedback. This feedback from fellow students and teachers should hopefully inspire them to take on new approaches and review their own working methods. Typical goals of any Moodle workshop include:

- Sharing good practice
- Adhering to agreed criteria
- Developing good peer assessment techniques
- Improving on a skill(s) through observation of different approaches

The workshop experience in Moodle has several stages which need to be understood before a successful one can be properly implemented for students to use effectively. When I set up a workshop, students need to:

- Submit an assignment to the workshop
- Perform a practice assessment of a similar assignment
- Understand the criteria to be assessed and the expectations placed upon them
- Conduct an assessment of an assignment(s) submitted to the workshop
- Receive assessments of their own work from other students in the group
- Receive assessments from the teacher of their assignment

A teacher setting up a workshop has control over many important elements in the experience including:

- The type of practice assessments a student conducts
- The number of practice assessments a student conducts
- The performance criteria to be assessed
- The number of real assessments to be conducted
- The allocation of real assessments to students
- The time scale for the workshop
- When the students receive the assessment results of their peers

The workshop is a valuable learning process. Students learn about the nature and complexity of their work. Teachers learn about the strengths and weaknesses of their students.

What to assess in a workshop?

Any work that can be submitted in an electronic format can be assessed in a workshop. Essay questions, slide presentations, podcasts, newspaper front pages, and so on can all be used as the material to assess within the workshop experience.

I have used workshops to assess:

Front page propaganda exercises about the execution of Charles I.

Presentations about 'Dunkirk – triumph or disaster?'

Podcasts about significant inventions of the Industrial Revolution.

Enquiry essays such as 'Would the Home Guard have made an effective fighting force against a German invasion during World War Two?'

It is important to have a clear idea of the assessment criteria. When planning the workshop, formulate clear ideas of the skills that you want your students to be able to perform in the actual piece of work and the skills that you want students to identify as part of the workshop. What skills do I want to concentrate on as the main outcomes of this workshop experience?

In this exercise, we would like our Year 7 students to create a presentation about the impact of the Black Death. We hope that they will use the presentation to discuss short-term as well as long-term consequences of the disease upon the country.

In our workshop, we are going to set up the opportunity for students to evaluate their own presentation against some marking criteria and also to evaluate the work of other students in the group. This will involve the opportunity to make some positive suggestions as to ways in which the assignment could have been improved. The more able children get to practise important evaluation skills. The weaker students get the chance to do this and also to look at the work of peers and perhaps consider approaches to use in future presentations. I find that students enjoy this activity because they are constructively engaged in criticism while also benefiting from the contributions of others.

In our exercise, students are going to submit their presentation about the Impact of the Black Death. This exercise has been done in conjunction with the ICT department who are interested in the students' ability to produce effective presentations with:

- Menus
- Different navigation options
- Evidence of spellchecking
- Evidence of proofreading
- Proper acknowledgement of sources

The assessment rubric will test these criteria if we set up each with statements such as:

Do navigation buttons work correctly on the menu screen?

The options to select might consist of:

- None work
- Some work
- Most work
- All work

Other statements might include:

Have the slides been spellchecked?

Have the slides been proofread?

Do the Home buttons work on all slides?

Are all sources properly acknowledged in the presentation?

The statements and answers are short and unambiguous. They can be tested and comments can be made on findings. The workshop is thus about students' understanding that good presentations follow clear guidelines . The presentation is also about historical content and knowledge. Students will compile a six-slide presentation about the topic and be prepared to present to peers either online or in front of their group. Discussion with colleagues helps to make the exercise cross-curricular.

Enabling the workshop module

If the Workshop module is absent from the **Add an activity** menu when editing is turned on, this will require consultation with the administrator to enable the module. This can be achieved using the following instructions:

1. Log in as administrator.
2. Click **Site administration**.
3. Click **Plugins**.
4. Click **Activity modules**.
5. Click **Manage activities**.
6. Unhide the 'eye' symbol beside the Workshop module.
7. Save any changes.
8. Log out as administrator.

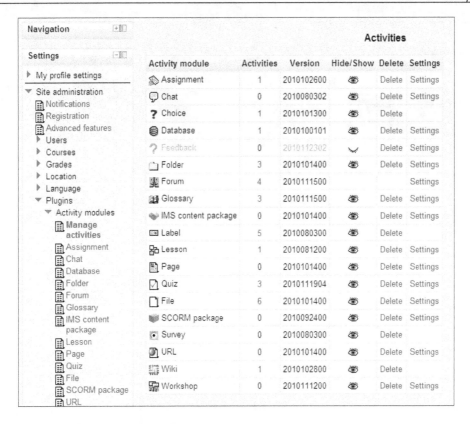

Creating a workshop

Our starting point is to create a workshop in **Topic 5 What was the impact of the Black Death?** Students may well have created their presentations, but they cannot submit them for assessment until the workshop has been created.

1. Open the Year 7 History course and turn on editing.

2. Click on **Add an activity** and select **Workshop**.

3. Enter the settings shown in the screenshot below:

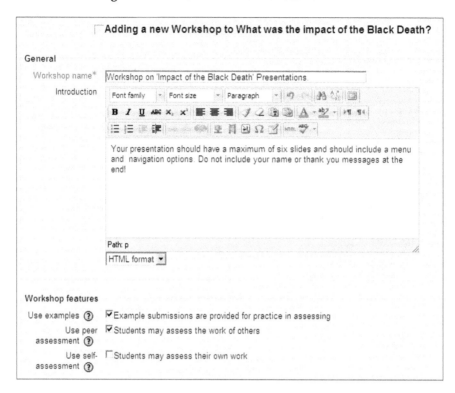

- ○ The **Workshop name** is important as this is the hyperlink that students will click on to enter the workshop. The title should be unambiguous.

- ○ The **Introduction** reminds students of some of the points we made at the start of the task. It acts as a last minute reminder that their work needs to meet certain guidelines established at the start of the exercise.

- ○ **Workshop features** includes three crucial checkboxes. **Use examples** must be checked because we shall give students a sample presentation to assess according to our marking criteria. **Use peer assessment** must also be checked because this is the key purpose of the whole process. We have left the **Use self- assessment** option unchecked because we do not want students to assess their own work. This option becomes important when allocating assignments to students for assessment.

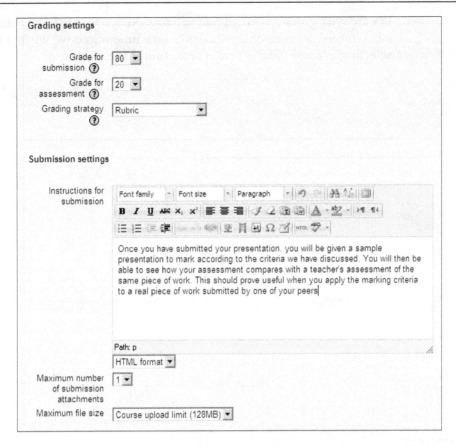

- ° We have set the **Grade for submission** and the **Grade for assessment** to show the weightings of the marks for the two tasks. We have selected **Rubric** for the **Grading strategy**, but we shall look at other strategies later. The actual rubric will be created in the next phase.

- ° **Submission settings** require some instructions to reassure students. It is not unusual for students to become concerned when they embark on a workshop for the first time. They may have questions and the **Instructions for submission** and later **Instructions for assessment** serve the useful purpose of informing students as they move through this process.

We are only going to accept one submission per student. We could have limited the size of the student's attachment had we wished by selecting a lower value from the **Maximum file size** dropdown.

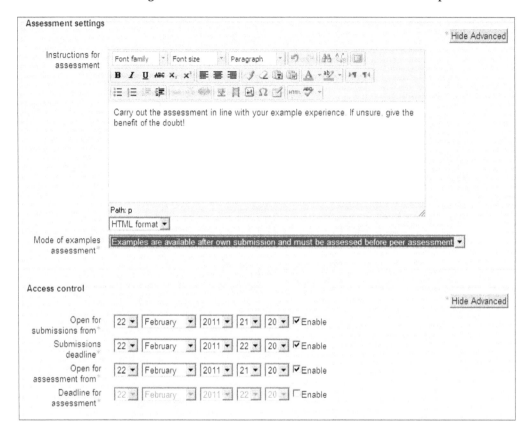

- ○ The **Mode of examples assessment** option is crucial for our particular workshop. We want students to complete their presentation and submit it to the workshop. Having done this, they will be stepped through the example exercise—rather like real examination moderation. Markers are not let loose on real work until they have had some training!

- ○ There are alternative routes to take under this option. It is a good idea to know which approach you wish to take before setting up the workshop. The other options include:

  - ○ **Assessment of example submission is voluntary**

  - ○ **Examples must be assessed before own submission**

○ **Access control** allows the teacher to set the dates by which assignments must be submitted and assessments marked—crucial for the success of a workshop. We have not imposed a time limit on assessments for this example because we only have three students and expect the assignments to be completed swiftly. It is not unusual for a teacher to return to this aspect of the **Setup phase** and extend deadlines so that work can be submitted, assessments performed, and so on. Students do not always adhere to deadlines!

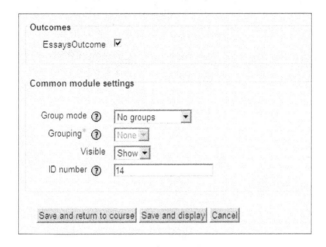

○ We have the option to include the task in our **EssaysOutcome** as the content could be evaluated in the same way as previous tasks. As it is also now an ICT task, there is a strong case for not including it.

○ **Common module settings** are important. We have seen how groups can be used with wikis. With a larger group, it might be appropriate here if **separate groups** was selected. Then students within the same group would only receive assignments from within their group.

4. Click **Save and return to course.**

○ If there appear to be a bewildering array of choices involved in setting up a workshop, then that is because there are and we are only half way through the process! The workshop module is not easy to master, but it is worthwhile and working through the list increases your awareness of the potential of the workshop. It is worth pursuing. We have chosen an option, the rubric for example, which precludes an assessor making comments about the marks they have awarded. We shall look at that option later.

Setting up the submission of student work

The next important stage requires the creation of the rubric we opted for—this is the means by which students will mark work. We also need to submit an example presentation for the students to practise with. Obviously time is saved if you know what you want the rubric to include and also have a sample presentation ready to use. I have learned over the years that considerable time is saved by planning for these elements before starting the workshop process.

1. Open the Year 7 History course and turn on editing.

2. Click on the workshop link now available in Topic 5.

3. Click **Edit workshop form** available in the **Setup Phase** of the table.

4. Enter the values as shown in the following screenshot:

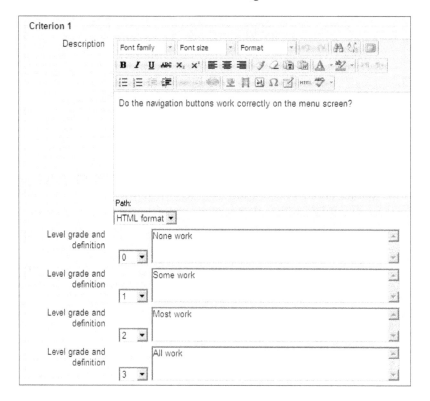

5. Complete the remaining four criterion in the same way.

6. Select **Grid** in the **Rubric layout** option:

   ° The grid is preferable to the list because a student would not need to scroll. It is an advantage to be able to see all options in this format on one screen.

7. Select **Save and preview** to view the grid as students would see it:

Assessment form				
Criteria	**Levels**			
Do the navigation buttons work correctly on the menu screen?	○ None work	○ Some work	○ Most work	○ All work
Have the slides been spellchecked?	○ None	○ Some	○ Most	○ All
Have the slides been proof read?	○ None	○ Some	○ Most	○ All
Do Home buttons work on slides?	○ None	○ Some	○ Most	○ All
Are sources acknowledged properly in the presentation?	○ None	○ Some	○ Most	○ All

8. Edit the grid using the edit options available until the form is as required.

9. Click **Save and close**.

Add example submission

The presentation that you wish students to practise their assessments on is now ready to be uploaded. It is a good idea to include obvious strengths and weaknesses in such a presentation. A button on the presentation that does not work helps to focus the minds of those who assess too quickly:

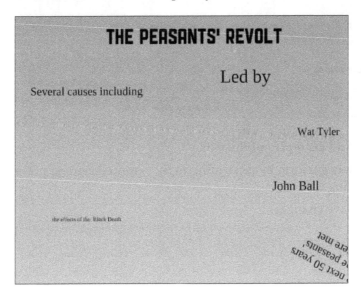

A student who submits a **prezi** rather than a conventional slide presentation has clearly completed the task, but not adhered to the ICT department's criteria. There will inevitably be some heated debate about how severe the marking should be! Small spelling or grammar errors help to encourage debate about when 'Some' and 'Most' should be used on the grid. These become useful discussion points about the importance of a thorough approach to assessment of another's work:

1. Click on the workshop link in **Topic 5**:

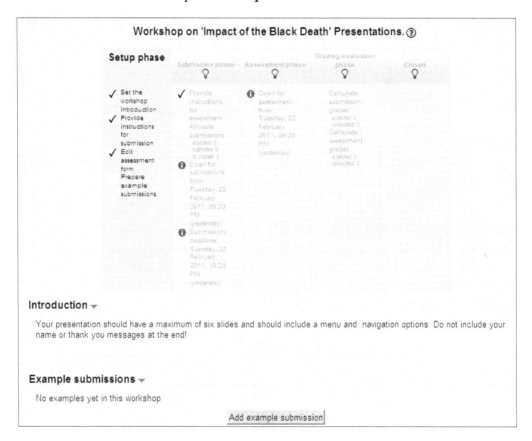

2. Click **Add example submission**.

3. Complete the form by navigating to the required sample presentation and uploading it.

4. Click **Save changes**:

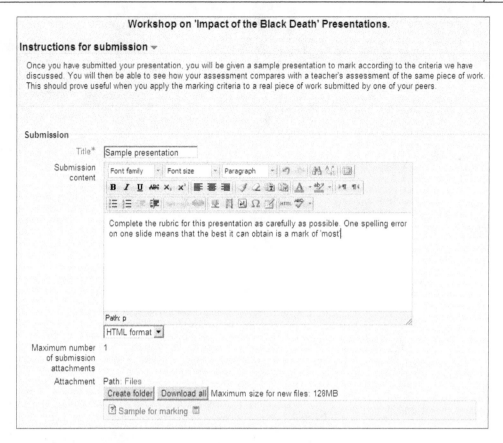

Provide a reference assessment

Having submitted the sample presentation, it is necessary to complete an assessment of it to provide a reference point for the workshop. Going back to the analogy of the examination markers, they are given a marking scheme with which to mark their scripts and similarly, the workshop needs an example of the marking scheme in action to compare with potentially different marks from students. When students assess the presentation, their marks should be in the same region or within a small margin of error.

1. Click the **Continue** option.
2. Click the **Assess example submission** button.
3. Open the sample presentation.
4. Use the **Rubric** grid to award marks.
5. Click **Save and close**.

6. The mark awarded for the presentation should be clearly visible in the bottom left-hand corner of the page:

The workshop is now ready for business if we switch from the **Setup phase** to the **Submission** phase. Once in that phase, students will be able to log in and submit their presentations for assessment. As soon as they have submitted, they will be eligible to perform the practice assessment and the real assessment.

Switching between workshop phases

1. Click the light bulb under **Submission phase**.

2. Click **Continue**.

3. Log out from the course.

You are about to switch the workshop into the **Submission phase**. Students may
submit their work during this phase (within the submission access control dates, if
set). Teachers may allocate submissions for peer review.

Continue   Cancel

Students submit presentations

Students can log in to the course and submit their presentation via the workshop
link. When BFoyle logs in and clicks on the workshop link, he will see the following
screen enabling him to submit his presentation via the hyperlink or **Submit** button:

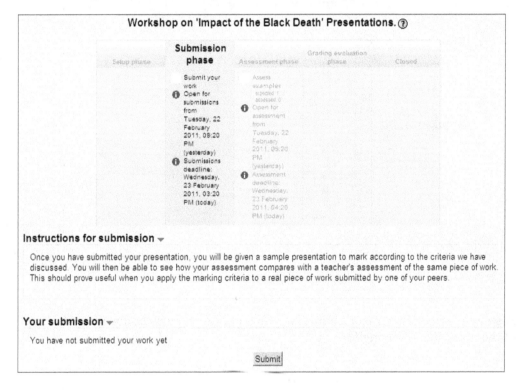

Instructions for submission ▾

Once you have submitted your presentation, you will be given a sample presentation to mark according to the criteria we have
discussed. You will then be able to see how your assessment compares with a teacher's assessment of the same piece of work.
This should prove useful when you apply the marking criteria to a real piece of work submitted by one of your peers.

Your submission ▾

You have not submitted your work yet

Submit

Clicking on the **Submit** button enables him to complete the familiar form that allows files to be uploaded. If BFoyle failed to submit his work by the deadline set in the workshop, the hyperlink would not be enabled and the **Submit** button would be absent. BFoyle would need to ask the teacher to extend the deadline that was originally set.

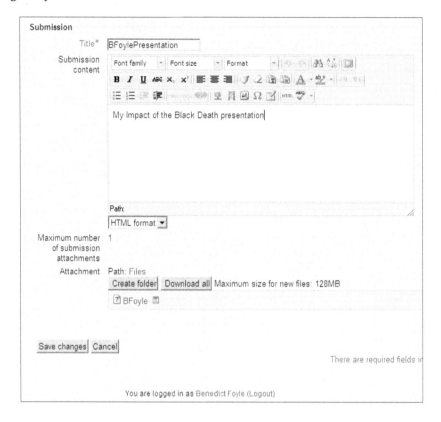

A student who submits work within the time period receives notification of receipt of the file in the following format:

Students perform example assessment

Students who have submitted their work are now ready to perform the practice assessment by themselves. When they log into the workshop, they are invited to do the practice assessment and when they submit their findings, they are able to compare their marks (in the second grid) with those of their teacher (in the first grid) for the same piece of work. In the example below, it can be seen that JFoyle has been far more generous than her teacher and, more importantly, where the discrepancies lie. JFoyle agreed with her teacher for the grading of the first and last statements in the rubric. On the second, third, and fourth statements however, she was more generous than her teacher and JFoyle's award of 64 is too high for this piece of work. A discussion between teacher and student about how the criteria have been applied would be invaluable. This would undoubtedly help her to assess more accurately when she encounters the real work of her peers in the next phase of the workshop task.

Criteria	Levels			
Do the navigation buttons work correctly on the menu screen?	( ) None work	( ) Some work	(x) Most work	( ) All work
Have the slides been spellchecked?	( ) None	(x) Some	( ) Most	( ) All
Have the slides been proof read?	( ) None	(x) Some	( ) Most	( ) All
Do Home buttons work on slides?	( ) None	( ) Some	(x) Most	( ) All
Are sources acknowledged properly in the presentation?	( ) None	( ) Some	(x) Most	( ) All

Assessment by yourself

Grade: 64 of 80

Criteria	Levels			
Do the navigation buttons work correctly on the menu screen?	( ) None work	( ) Some work	(x) Most work	( ) All work
Have the slides been spellchecked?	( ) None	( ) Some	( ) Most	(x) All
Have the slides been proof read?	( ) None	( ) Some	(x) Most	( ) All
Do Home buttons work on slides?	( ) None	( ) Some	( ) Most	(x) All
Are sources acknowledged properly in the presentation?	( ) None	( ) Some	(x) Most	( ) All

Allocating assignments to students

The teacher has the opportunity to allocate assignments to students to assess. This needs to be done in the **Submission** phase using the **Allocate** link. We would like each presentation to be marked by each of the other two workshop participants. We can ensure this by performing a manual allocation ourselves:

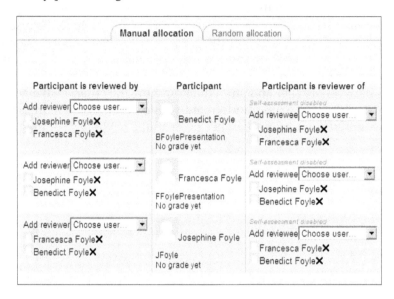

When setting up the workshop, we deliberately disabled the self-assessment option. We could achieve the same outcome using the random allocation tab and selecting **2** as the number of allocations:

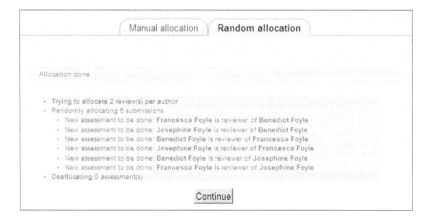

Students perform the peer assessment

When each student logs in to the course, they will see two presentations to open. They must then perform an assessment on each presentation according to the guidelines learned in the sample exercise.

Thus when BFoyle logs in to the course, he sees the links to two presentations that need to be assessed. Clicking on the **Assess** button will open up the **Rubric** grid:

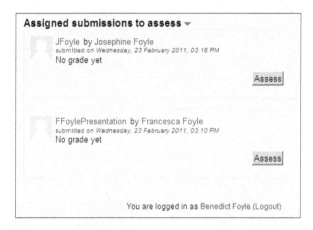

Analysing the results of the workshop

When all assessments have been completed by all participants, we can switch to the final phase of the workshop, the **Grading evaluation** phase. Here the results can be collated and analysed. This is achieved by switching on the light bulb in the fourth column.

A look at the scores shows some interesting results:

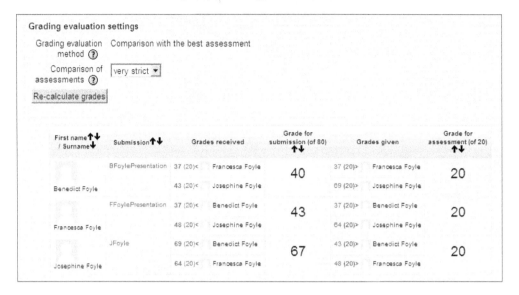

The best presentation was by JFoyle. It obtained the two highest marks awarded by her peers and she earned a total of (67 + 20) or 87 out of 100. The weakest presentation was by BFoyle.

How reliable was the assessing? You will notice that we set the **Comparison of assessments** to the **very strict** level. If there were wide discrepancies between the scores for an assessment, then this would reduce the mark scored for that presentation. As the scores for particular presentations tended to be closely aligned, this would suggest that the assessments by participants were in line with the marking scheme and hence the participants have scored maximum marks (20 marks out of a possible 20 marks) in this aspect of the task. Clearly they have appreciated that good presentations use clear navigation, careful spellchecking and proofreading, and concise acknowledgement of sources. The presentations were not bad either!

How do teachers assess in a workshop?

Teachers can assess work submitted by their students by clicking on the file submission itself and selecting the **Assess** button:

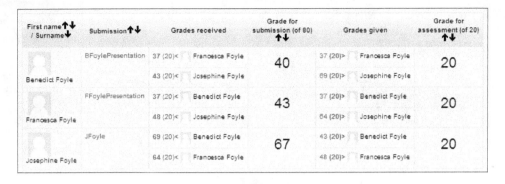

First name↑↓ / Surname↓	Submission↑↓	Grades received		Grade for submission (of 80) ↑↓	Grades given		Grade for assessment (of 20) ↑↓
Benedict Foyle	BFoylePresentation	37 (20)<	Francesca Foyle	40	37 (20)>	Francesca Foyle	20
		43 (20)<	Josephine Foyle		69 (20)>	Josephine Foyle	
Francesca Foyle	FFoylePresentation	37 (20)<	Benedict Foyle	43	37 (20)>	Benedict Foyle	20
		48 (20)<	Josephine Foyle		64 (20)>	Josephine Foyle	
Josephine Foyle	JFoyle	69 (20)<	Benedict Foyle	67	43 (20)>	Benedict Foyle	20
		64 (20)<	Francesca Foyle		48 (20)>	Francesca Foyle	

The assessment form will appear in exactly the same way with the addition of the following element:

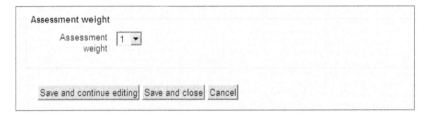

It makes sense to adjust the weighting of a teacher's assessment of a piece of work. Changing the **Assessment weight** to 2, for example, means that this mark counts towards the student's average (out of 80) as if two people had submitted the same assessment. Changing it to **16** means that **16** people would have submitted a similar mark. This gives teachers the power to influence overall marks to a considerable extent. If this is a good mark, it has a beneficial effect on the overall mark and if it is a poor mark, it has a similarly negative impact.

Continuing down the form, the teacher can also make an impact upon the assessments that students have performed on each other:

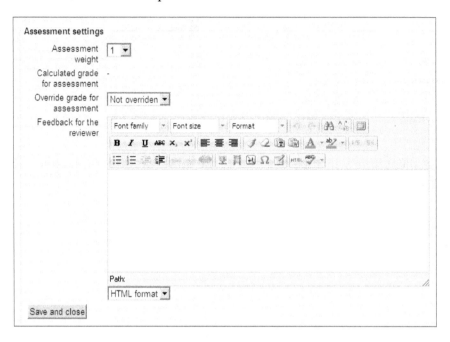

If we apply the same logic, a teacher could give a strong student assessor an increased weighting, thus influencing the second value (out of 20) shown in our grading analysis. A teacher can override a grade given by a student and there is space to provide feedback to the reviewer.

What happens to BFoyle's grade when we include my marking of the submissions? At present, his grade stands at 40 because it is the average of the two grades he has received. I have decided that my assessing should carry more weight than my students' assessments. My assessing is therefore weighted at 2, compared to student assessments which have a weighting of 1:

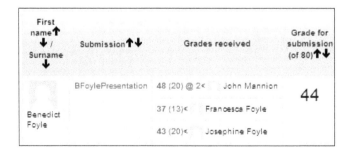

I assessed BFoyle's submission, giving it a grade of 48, receiving the grading grade of 20 for my assessment. The effect on BFoyle's overall mark is to move it from 40 to 44. This grade is the average of the four grades: 48, 48, 37, and 43. The grade, if the teacher's assessment had a weighting of 3, would be the average of 48, 48, 48, 37, and 43, which would have given BFoyle a grade of 45. Clearly teachers' use of weighting influences the assessment procedure and ensures the integrity of the assessments.

FFoyle's grading shows that she awarded BFoyle a grade of 37. She received a grading grade of 13. The < symbol indicates that I have accepted this grading. Had FFoyle's grading appeared as 37 (13/11)>, it would indicate that I had decided to use the **Override grade for assessment** dropdown to reduce it to 11. I would have provided feedback in the textbox to indicate to her why I felt she was marking too strictly. The form enables teachers to intervene to preserve the integrity of the assessment procedure and alert students if they are being too generous or too strict. In many ways, it mimics the online marking systems that many examination boards have adopted in the UK.

Different types of grading strategy

What other types of grading strategy could we use for our 'Impact of the Black Death' presentations? We could make our assessment form purely comment driven if we wanted to by selecting the **Comments** option instead of **Rubric** on the workshop's **Grading strategy** dropdown on the **Settings** page.

The first question in the form would resemble the following screenshot:

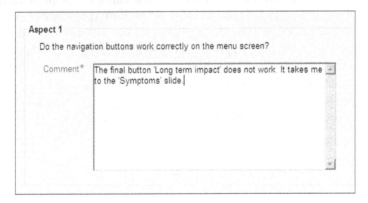

Reviewers can give detailed feedback in the textbox about a student's performance in the presentation.

Another option is to set the **Grading strategy** to **Number of errors.** This option is useful if you want your students to answer Yes or No to the question and the final grade is a calculation based upon the number of positive responses. Questions can be weighted to give them a higher value than others. If, in our example, the ICT teacher wanted extra value to be placed on the questions about spellchecking, proofreading, and acknowledgement of sources, this can be done as the question is being set up. If we look at Question 2, the setup phase would look like this:

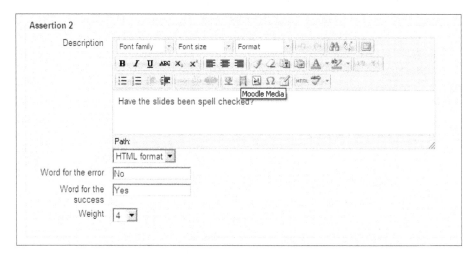

Having the answer marked as No would lose 20% of available marks, but having a weighting of **4** means that this answer carries more value to the final mark than a question with a weighting of **1**. Students who do well on questions 2, 3, and 5 will score higher marks than those who do well on questions 1 and 4. At the bottom of this form, the table of percentages, given that there are five questions accounting for 20% each of the available marks, will look like the following screenshot. The percentages to the right can be safely ignored:

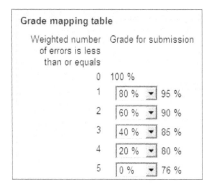

The following screenshot is an example of the assessment form which is filled in by participants in the workshop:

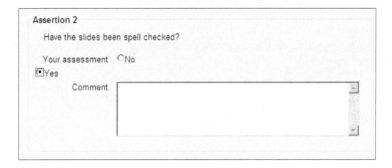

That leaves us with one last **grading strategy – accumulative grading.** This option allows us to set marks, set weights, and add comments, but the awarding of marks is not as prescriptive as the previous method. During the editing of the assessment form, Question 2 would resemble the following screenshot:

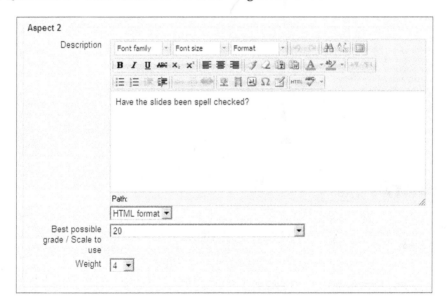

I have allocated questions 2, 3, and 5 a possible 20 marks each to raise their profile and given them a weighting of 4 as opposed to 1. Thus the ICT teacher's wishes have been respected and those students who score well on proof reading, spell checking, and acknowledging sources will see this reflected in their overall scores compared to those who only score highly on questions that rely on efficient use of ICT wizardry!

The assessment form which students see would resemble the following screen:

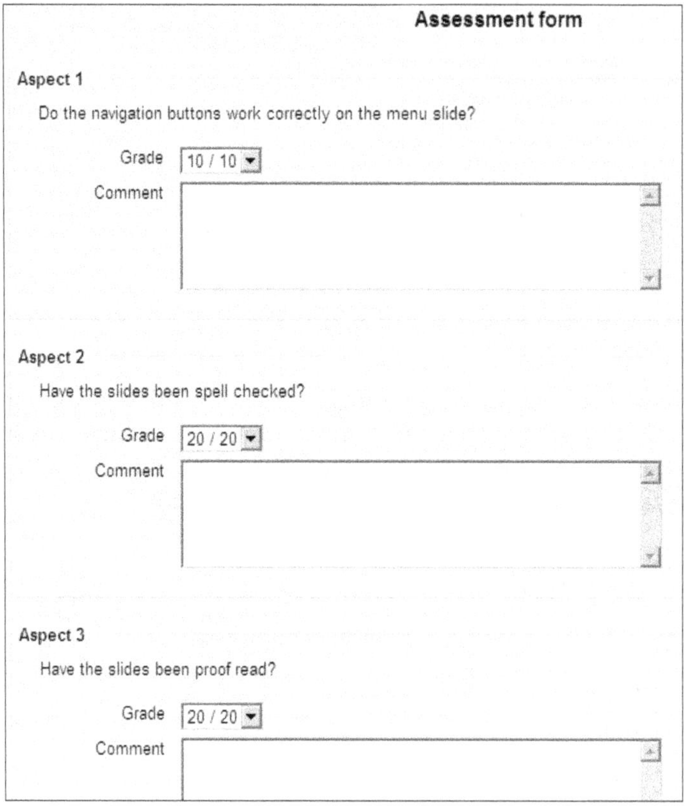

Assessment form

Aspect 1

Do the navigation buttons work correctly on the menu slide?

Grade   10 / 10 ▾

Comment

Aspect 2

Have the slides been spell checked?

Grade   20 / 20 ▾

Comment

Aspect 3

Have the slides been proof read?

Grade   20 / 20 ▾

Comment

Backup

As the creator and teacher of this course, you will want to be able to keep a backup copy for disaster recovery purposes and for use in the following academic year. If you go into **Settings** and **Course administration**, you will see the **Backup** link. Backing up the Year 7 History course involves a four stage process which is not nearly as complicated as that might sound.

Clicking the **Backup** link opens the **Initial settings** stage:

The boxes that are ticked are the elements that you have permission to back up. If you wish to back up anything else, then you are going to have to negotiate with your administrator. The settings as they stand are sufficient to restore the course for use at the start of the following academic year without any of the user data from this year.

Clicking the **Next** button opens the **Schema settings** stage:

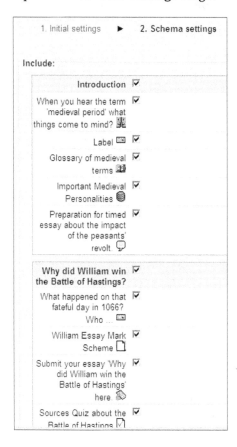

The screenshot shows each of the different items that will be backed up in the file that is going to be created. Again there will be confirmation that user data will not be included. Clicking **Next** opens the third stage:

The next stage allows you to change the file name of the backup file and to make any last minute changes. You will now need to click the **Perform backup** button:

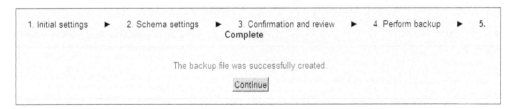

On completion of the backup you should see a message confirming that the backup has been completed successfully. Click **Continue** to find out where the file has been saved and how to make a copy of the backup to an external drive.

Backing up to an external drive

The course file that has been backed up can be clearly identified by the date and time. To back up this file on an external drive, click the **Download** button beside it, navigate to the required storage area and click **Save**:

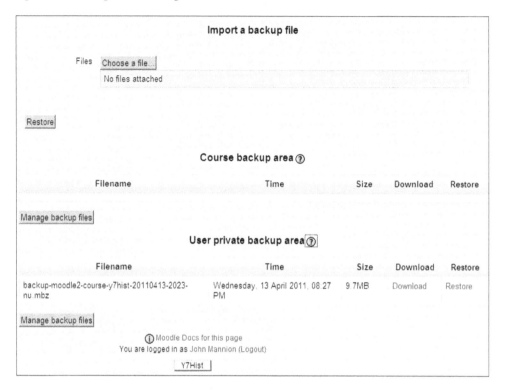

Restoring the Year 7 History course

If you go into **Settings** and **Course administration**, you will see the **Restore** link. To restore the Year 7 History course:

1. Click the **Choose a file** button.

2. Click **Recent files** in the file picker or navigate to an alternative saved location via **Upload a file**.

3. Select the file.

4. Click the **Select this file** button in the **file picker**.

5. Click the **Restore** button:

6. As with the backup process, there are several stages and buttons to click before progressing from one stage to the next:

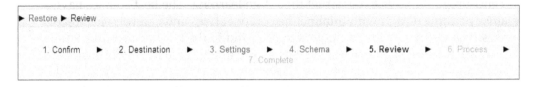

7. Await a confirmation message that the file has been restored successfully.

8. You can now test the course to see that the correct elements are all in place.

Administrator rights are much more powerful with respect to backing up and restoring permissions.

Summary

The workshop is worth exploring because of the value of peer-to-peer assessment to your students. Having come this far with the use of Moodle in the teaching of History, the workshop is an Aladdin's Cave of options and experiences for your students—some heartening, some chastening, but all valuable in the context of learning how to learn. It is an innovative, diagnostic, and truly cross-curricular tool.

Immediate success with workshops involves:

- Knowing your assessment requirements from the start
- Knowing the grading strategy to impose
- Making appropriate use of weighting
- Framing simple, smart questions
- Having an appropriate sample exercise

Longer term success with workshops involves:

- Being prepared to switch between phases to adjust deadlines
- Experimenting with the order in which tasks are undertaken
- Finding out how to make assessors anonymous
- Producing league tables of results

It is appropriate to conclude with this chapter because the workshop encapsulates so much that is wonderful about using Moodle in the teaching of History. Students collaborate in the workshop to learn new skills and techniques or share good practice. Other tools that we have looked at encourage similar collaboration and encourage students to construct their own learning. The best courses have a relatively simple design with minimal use of font styles and careful selection of images. The real magic for students is to be found in the teacher-inspired activities with quizzes, forums, glossaries, databases, and assignments. Moodle enables creative and dynamic learning to take place with a relatively small investment of time. In the constantly changing world of education that makes it priceless.

Index

Thank you for buying
History Teaching with Moodle 2

About Packt Publishing

Packt, pronounced 'packed', published its first book "*Mastering phpMyAdmin for Effective MySQL Management*" in April 2004 and subsequently continued to specialize in publishing highly focused books on specific technologies and solutions.

Our books and publications share the experiences of your fellow IT professionals in adapting and customizing today's systems, applications, and frameworks. Our solution based books give you the knowledge and power to customize the software and technologies you're using to get the job done. Packt books are more specific and less general than the IT books you have seen in the past. Our unique business model allows us to bring you more focused information, giving you more of what you need to know, and less of what you don't.

Packt is a modern, yet unique publishing company, which focuses on producing quality, cutting-edge books for communities of developers, administrators, and newbies alike. For more information, please visit our website: www.packtpub.com.

About Packt Open Source

In 2010, Packt launched two new brands, Packt Open Source and Packt Enterprise, in order to continue its focus on specialization. This book is part of the Packt Open Source brand, home to books published on software built around Open Source licences, and offering information to anybody from advanced developers to budding web designers. The Open Source brand also runs Packt's Open Source Royalty Scheme, by which Packt gives a royalty to each Open Source project about whose software a book is sold.

Writing for Packt

We welcome all inquiries from people who are interested in authoring. Book proposals should be sent to author@packtpub.com. If your book idea is still at an early stage and you would like to discuss it first before writing a formal book proposal, contact us; one of our commissioning editors will get in touch with you.

We're not just looking for published authors; if you have strong technical skills but no writing experience, our experienced editors can help you develop a writing career, or simply get some additional reward for your expertise.

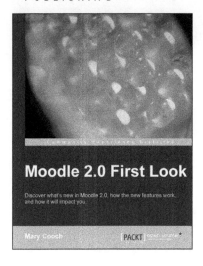

Moodle 2.0 First Look

ISBN: 978-1-849511-94-0   Paperback: 272 pages

Discover what's new in Moodle 2.0, how the new features work, and how it will impact you

1. Get an insight into the new features of Moodle 2.0

2. Discover the benefits of brand new additions such as Comments and Conditional Activities

3. Master the changes in administration with Moodle 2.0

4. The first and only book that covers all of the fantastic new features of Moodle 2.0

Moodle 2.0 Multimedia Cookbook

ISBN: 978-1-849514-70-5   Paperback: 256 pages

Add images, videos, music, and much more to make your Moodle course interactive and fun

1. Learn how to add photographs, videos, animations, and much more to make your Moodle course even more interactive

2. Embed 2D or 3D maps, interactive or static charts, resources, assets, videos, bitmaps, and photographs into Moodle courses

3. Learn how to design and work with podcasts, audio assets, sound, music, and screencasts and integrate them into Moodle

Please check **www.PacktPub.com** for information on our titles

www.ingramcontent.com/pod-product-compliance
Lightning Source LLC
Chambersburg PA
CBHW080358060326

40689CB00019B/4057